A
CHRISTIAN
VIEW OF
JUSTICE

A CHRISTIAN VIEW OF JUSTICE

Mark T. Coppenger

BROADMAN PRESS
Nashville, Tennessee

4261-26
ISBN: 0-8054-6126-4

Dewey Decimal Classification: 261.8
Subject headings: CHURCH AND SOCIAL PROBLEMS / / JUSTICE
Library of Congress Catalog Card Number: 82-70867
Printed in the United States of America

To my earthly father,

Raymond Arthur Coppenger

Preface

This book originated in my perplexity during the Nixon-McGovern race of 1973. I was pulled in many directions by the competing claims of the campaign and was uncomfortable in my confusion. My interest in answers grew as I was drawn into a variety of arguments and conversations on public policy.

When, as a new faculty member at Wheaton College, I joined a summer seminar on the integration of faith and learning, I was pleased to hear my paper assignment. The requirement that I explore the connection between my discipline, philosophy, and my Christian faith, perfectly served my need for work on justice. So began my inquiry.

Through the next five years, the college supported this study in many ways—the Alumni Association funded a quarter's leave for writing; my colleagues, Arthur Holmes, Steve Evans, and David Schlafer, worked thoughtfully through the manuscript with me; typists, Rose Sandstrom, Joy Houston, and Betty Goddard, served graciously and carefully; Academic Vice-Presidents Donald Mitchell and Ward Kriegbaum gave me strategic support; the *Wheaton Alumni* let me sketch my theory before its readers; my students in Philosophy of Law gave me their thoughts on the project; an anonymous benefactor encouraged me with a cash gift through the alumni office. So my debt to Wheaton College is enormous.

Our church, Glenfield Baptist of Glen Ellyn, also figured into the picture. We spent two weeks of our study leave at the home of old Vanderbilt friends, the Gaedes, in Massachusetts. When we'd just arrived, word came that our home was facing serious water damage from the blizzard of '79. Within a few hours of our evening call for help, church friends were on our roof and in our house, shoveling, chipping, and cleaning up. Because of the emergency work of the Dickersons, Greers, Odells, and Wests, and, from the college, the Kriegbaums and Bartels, we were able to work on in Massachusetts and to find our home intact when we returned.

Sharon, my wife, as always supplied a sympathetic ear, good counsel, and encouragement. My mother Agnes Coppenger, gave the manuscript a close and skillful reading.

I hate to associate all these good names with the errors this book may contain. But I would hate even more not thanking these friends for their kind help.

Contents

Introduction 11

1 God, the Father 15
  Fatherhood 15
  Consequentialists and Obligists 16
  God and the Consequentialist 18
  Happiness 20
  The Bible and Human Nature 21
  Alternative Life-styles 22
  God's Promises 22
  Cooperation with God 23
  Cooperation with Nonbelievers 25
  Justice, a Part of Goodness 26

2 Desert 28
  The Common View of Retribution 28
  A Brief Sketch of the Theory 29
  Rules and Desert 31
  God and the Rules 33
  Salubrious Retribution 34
  Desert and Action 35
  Desert and Qualification 37
  Persons 38
  A Continuum 40
  Responsibility 41
  Children and the Mentally Ill 42
  Ascription 43
  Harm and Benefit 46
  Freedom and Happiness 47

3 A Matrix 48
  Deserved Harm 48
  Punishment and the New Testament 51
  A Division of Labor 53
  Mercy 55
  The *Lex Talionis* 55
  The Fool 58
  Happiness and the Fool 60
  Victims 65
  Public and Private Sectors 67
  Deserved Benefit 69

Just Wage 70
Stewards 72
Undeserved Benefit 73
Wealth 74
The Lesser Evil 75
The Firing Squad Case 78
The Brinks Case 80
Just Means 82
A Straw Man 82
Finitude 84
Summary 85
Equality 85
Rights 86

4 Statute and Administrative Law 90
Taxation 91
Wages 97
Welfare 103
Prices 108
Health Care 119
Foreign Aid 127
War 129
Public Education 138

5 Case Law 140
De Funis vs. Odegaard
Supreme Court of Washington (1973)
(Reverse Discrimination) 141

Buck vs. Bell
United States Supreme Court (1927)
(Sterilization of Retarded Persons) 147

Paris Adult Theatre vs. Slaton
United States Supreme Court (1973)
(Pornography) 151

Nader vs. General Motors Corporation
Court of Appeals of New York (1970)
(Invasion of Privacy) 156

Kaimowitz vs. Department of Mental Health for
the State of Michigan in the Circuit Court
for the County of Wayne (1973)
(Psychosurgery) 162

Conclusion 172

Introduction

This is not a careful word study. Neither is it a careless word study. It is, instead, an educated guess about what the Bible has to say to those who would make public policy. It would be wonderfully comforting if the Bible were so written as to eliminate the guesswork, but it is not. This too invites guesswork. Why did God provide us with Scripture which can serve both the John Birch Society and the Amish? Of course, a good deal of the controversy surrounding the Scriptures can be attributed to selective and perverse reading. But this is not the whole story. There are significant disagreements among earnest and decent students of the Bible.

The fact of and not the reason for this confusion is pertinent to this work. It is mentioned both to qualify and to defend what follows. First for the qualification. A reasonable person can reject this work. The theory does not fall from the pages of Scripture in such a way as to silence all but the most willful critics. It is a guess. That should be enough qualification.

Now for the defense. Any biblical interpretation of this scope must admit to the same qualifications if it is to be honest. The diversity of the passages makes construal of the whole uncertain.

For better or worse the student of Scripture must stand back and make an embarrassingly tenuous guess. And regardless of how satisfying and persuasive this guess may prove to be, he must not forget that it is, at base, a guess.

What proof is there for this one? Which verses establish it as true? None of them and all of them. The same should be the case for any general account of the biblical message. The lonely proof text makes for bad doctrine, and one person's proof text is another's hard saying. Each theory has its point of discomfort. Each sits comfortably upon some verses while gingerly touching others. So while the charge that a passage resists natural accommodation to a certain theory counts, it is not enough to destroy the theory. Each theory must work at interpreting this or that verse in a somewhat strained fashion. Why this is so is perplexing. That it is so is undeniable. So neither proof nor disproof will succeed at the single verse level. Instead, the theory has to be judged as a system, as over against other systems.

The first three chapters construct an interpretive framework; they attempt a fair account of the basics of biblical justice. The categorical matrix which emerges frames the discussion of specifics in the next two chapters. These last chapters contain detailed verdicts based upon general principles.

This then is the program—a guess plus applications. It is briefly executed in hope that the reader will not bog down, that he will get the overall picture as soon as possible. For it is primarily a system, a concoction, and not a tribute to ingredients. There is plenty of time for development, refinement, and correction if the general impression is favorable. If it is not, then the reader will be spared those details.

In framing a biblical theory of justice, it won't do to build strictly upon those passages which contain words translated "just" and "justice." This is so for several reasons. First, there is not a clear fit between today's question of justice and one biblical sense of the word. In some translations, justice and righteousness are the same. Consider the King James Version of Ezekiel 18:5-9:

But if a man be just, and do that which is lawful and right, And hath not eaten upon the mountains, neither hath lifted up his eyes to the idols of the house of Israel, neither hath defiled his neighbour's wife, neither hath come near to a menstruous woman, And hath not oppressed any, but hath restored to the debtor his pledge, hath spoiled none by violence, hath given his bread to the hungry, and hath covered the naked with a garment; He that hath not given forth upon usury, neither hath taken any increase, that hath withdrawn his hand from iniquity, hath executed true judgment between man and man, Hath walked in my statutes, and hath kept my judgments, to deal truly; he is just, he shall surely live, saith the Lord God.

Here the word *just* covers the whole of virtue—piety, integrity, compassion, restraint, lawfulness. To be just is to be good. It is to be worthy of the most general form of praise.

When we, today, speak of justice, our focus is not upon the consummately good man. Instead, we are concerned with matters of state. What is a good law? What government programs are acceptable? Of course, it is important to discover what's involved in being a good person. But it is also important to decide what makes for good public policy. In deciding the latter, we must not be confused by passages which address the former.

Second, when the passage points to public policy rather than personal righteousness, we do not find the sort of summary working principle we seek. Psalm 82:2-3 is typical:

> How long will you judge unjustly
> and show partiality to the wicked?
> Give justice to the weak and the fatherless;
> maintain the right of the afflicted and the destitute.

We see here that justice somehow involves fair play for all alike, what we call "due process" and "equal protection." But this can't serve as our only guideline. The concept "due process" does not exhaust the question of public policy. We know we're not supposed to pervert justice for the sake of a bribe or out of disdain for the wretched. But what exactly is this thing justice which we are not to pervert? Psalm 82:2-3 does not say, nor do other verses which speak of justice.

Third, the Bible says a good deal about public policy without using "just" or its cognates at all:

> You shall not oppress your neighbor or rob him. The wages of a hired

servant shall not remain with you all night until the morning (Lev. 19:13).

If there is a dispute between men, and they come into court, and the judges decide between them, acquitting the innocent and condemning the guilty, then if the guilty man deserves to be beaten, the judge shall cause him to lie down and be beaten in his presence with a number of stripes in proportion to his offense (Deut. 25:1-2).

The task is, then, one of sorting through a wide variety of passages, some mentioning justice, some not. This is tricky business. In one place, God directs the death penalty for adultery (Lev. 20:10), while in another he protects an adulterous woman from injury (John 8:1-11). And in no place do we find reference to the issues of tax-free status for churches, reverse discrimination, or the use of nuclear weapons. The Bible is not as categorically accessible as the yellow pages. But I hope to demonstrate that there is implicit in Scripture all the public policy guidance we need.

1
God, the Father

Fatherhood

In framing this model of justice, we begin by considering the metaphor God the Father which appears scores of times in the Bible. God is pictured as Father to the people of Israel (1 Chron. 29:10), Father of the fatherless (Ps. 68:5), an everlasting Father in Christ (Isa. 9:6), and the Father of Christ (Matt. 3:17). To understand the words of God, it is helpful to unpack the notion of fatherhood.

There is, of course, a procreative sense of fatherhood; God, our Father, is the source of our being, both physically and spiritually. But more than this, we bear a family resemblance to him; we are made in his image (Gen. 1:26). That is to say, as persons who value, will, and act, we are like God. We were not, in the first place, aliens, though we came to be alienated from him. Still, there is opportunity for reconciliation which serves to uncover and redeem our original Godlike natures.

The fatherhood of God goes beyond generation to the realities of family life. The normal father exhibits love for his children. The scriptural accounts fit nicely, for the references to and illustrations of God's love are plentiful. Of these references, one stands out as ultimate, 1 John 4:8: "He who does not love does not know God; for God is love."

It is well known that the love of God is not fatuous or sentimental; it is intelligent love of the caliber found only in an omniscient being. As a loving Father, God shows both tenderness and sternness; there is a time to embrace and a time to discipline. A father whose orders are strictly self-serving, a matter of convenience, is not genuinely loving. The child often thinks the father's directives pointless or pernicious, but the child of a loving father is just that, a child. He lacks the perspective to understand the rules. Naps, cleanliness, and politeness are just so much annoyance. Only when the child matures does he have the background to appreciate the rules. A two-year-old cannot handle the concepts of amebic dysentery and social order. Still the loving father constrains the child to behave as though he did understand.

The father compels the child to respect the interests of the family while taking care to accommodate the child's individual interests. Indeed he understands that the well-being of the family is in the individual child's best interest. No loving rule confounds the child for the sake of the family or confounds the family for the sake of the child. The interests are congruent, intertwined. Whatever measure of liberty or limit the father imposes, he has in mind the well-being of the family and its members. When a father forbids a practice, he does so with the understanding that the practice destroys or undermines. When he refrains from laying down rules, he does so with the understanding that there is legitimate leeway in the selection of fruitful life-styles. And whatever the rules, they do not have the character of alien decrees, of bizarre standards which bear no relationship to the demands of the human condition. A loving father's commands are not a Procrustean bed. Rather, the rules are the way to the child's well-being. So, too, are the commands of God, the Father.

This talk of God the father is not meant as a snub to feminists. A mother's instructions to her child are also loving and wise. The choice of expression merely reflects that of Scripture without judging its suitability for today. For that issue lies beyond this present project.

Consequentialists and Obligists

Two broad categories of ethical thought, teleology and deontology, warrant attention in this chapter. The first focuses upon consequences, the second upon duty. Each is, in large measure, a reaction to an abomination. The teleologist gives the Scylla of legalism wide berth, while the deontologist stears clear of the Charybdis of expediency.

The teleologist, or consequentialist as we shall call him, considers the value of an act in terms of results. What leads to unsurpassed net happiness? How can we achieve the greatest balance of pleasure over pain? These are the sorts of questions judged most pertinent to ethical decision-making. If a rule is more of a hardship than a blessing, then it is a poor rule. If social structures demand more of men than they give, then they are rejected. If a moral code stifles those who follow it, then it fails.

From the consequentialist's viewpoint, legalists and moral fanatics are abominable. What could be sadder than a person no longer sensitive to the happiness of his fellows? Obsessed with duty or rules, he tramples on feelings, ignores dire consequences, and makes life intolerable for those he encounters. His inflexibility is infuriating. He is, in short, a Pharisee.

The other perspective belongs to the deontologist, or, to coin a word, the obligist. (The 'de' in deontology comes from the Greek expression *dei* meaning "it is necessary.") He is most sensitive to duty. He recognizes that moral choices can be difficult and demanding, that virtue is not always pleasurable, and that sacrifice has its day. One's station, promises, and very humanity require certain behavior of him. And whether or not there is promise of gain, he presses on to do what is right.

For him, expediency is abominable. He finds those who would justify means on the basis of ends alone contemptible. He fears that life and duty will be trampled in the rush for happiness and group comfort. In his view, there are no limits to what a consequentialist might do if the circumstances, the prospects for personal or social gain, are right—kill innocents, break promises, betray friends.

When the consequentialist and the obligist duel, they remind each other of these abominations, and rightfully so. Pharisaism and expediency are both objectionable. Each of the parties, of course, has a defense against his special danger. The consequentialist argues that expediency is bad policy in that it generates more grief than happiness. And he notes that his system generates duty just as surely as his critic's; it is one's often uncomfortable duty to pursue the best consequences. The obligist claims that beneficence, concern for human well-being, is one of his obligations, and that happiness is a by-product of virtue. Both show their interest in human well-being and devotion to duty. Neither wants unhappiness and lawlessness. Their division comes over the question of priorities.

What, then, of the "father model" of ethics? Is it consequentialist or obligist? With all its emphasis upon human well-being, it is a consequentialist theory. But the father theorist does not act as though he were a consequentialist. Instead, his behavior matches that of a particular kind of obligist, the divine command theorist. He treats God's Word as law; he doesn't demand to know the results before he submits to God's directives. Indeed, he may act in a fashion which is apparently at odds with happiness. He may give a tithe to God's work despite the fact that he is too poor to live comfortably. He may even refuse to steal to feed his starving family. Unlike many of his consequentialist brothers, he is not one to insist upon making or seeing the happiness calculations before he acts.

God and the Consequentialist

It would be a mistake for the child to reason as follows: "Father, who knows best, wills our happiness in framing rules, so I should base my own ethical judgments upon my estimation of the consequences in terms of human happiness." For the child may lack that essential ingredient, knowledge, which underlies a wise decision. What seems right to the child may well lead to serious difficulties, difficulties he could have foreseen if he had had the father's experience. The father is an epistemic authority for the child. How much more is God an epistemic authority for his children. His knowledge is without gaps. Anyone who chooses to ignore the directives of God the Father is analogous to a patient who snatches the scalpel from the surgeon's hand and insists upon performing the operation himself, without medical training. Of course the patient is bold and self-reliant, but he is also a fool. Smart people do not put their faith in the wrong people, themselves or other pretending authorities. They accept the work of, to use another familiar metaphor, the Great Physician. The consequentialist errs, then, when he insists upon making the happiness calculations himself or upon trusting the calculations of other finite minds. His strength lies in his recognition of the ultimate humanity of ethical rules; his weakness is his determination to let humans, other children if you will, formulate the rules.

But doesn't the father theorist find himself in an impious position? Hasn't he recognized a moral standard other than God himself? Is he not saying that God's commands must serve human well-being if they are to be acceptable? Doesn't this mean that God could conceivably be immoral? Yes or no, depending upon the sense you attach to the word, conceivable. If by the word you mean "a live possibility," then the immorality of God is inconceivable. If, though, you mean "thinkable without contradiction," then God is conceivably immoral. For example, we can imagine a malevolent God wishing to annoy and destroy humans for amusement. Surely we would not call this a moral God. But it could be objected, "God could not be this way, for God is a loving God. Indeed, God just means 'loving creator of the universe.' So it is inconceivable that God be malevolent." The argument, at this point, simply becomes one of definition. I use the word *God* to denote simply the person who created and rules the world. In this sense God could be evil. The creator of us all could be anti-man rather than pro-man. He is not, though, and this is reason to praise him. If he had been malevolent, he would not have been worthy of our praise and obedience. Just because he created us and has power over us, it does not follow logically that he is good.

Happiness

What precisely is this standard by which we measure even God? It's not clear that there is a precise standard, but imprecisely we may speak of human happiness and well-being. Though we do not consciously seek it in most of our choices, the desire to be happy lies behind our day-to-day choices. We size up life and select a certain life-style, trusting it to bring and sustain satisfaction. If the life-style fails to bring satisfaction, then we may well abandon it after giving it a thorough try. We are all familiar with cases like that of the accountant who leaves the big city for a simple, farming life in the country, the couple in their fifties who divorce after thirty years of marriage, the conservative churchgoer who becomes a swinger, the swinger who becomes a devout believer. Upon reflection, they find their old lives unfulfilling and adopt a new plan. Many people change life-styles as though they were seasonal clothing and chase after every latest self-help scheme. Their demand for quick results can kill even the best prospects. Most of us are more patient, but we all seek something to bring us enduring satisfaction. And if we do not, in the long run, find it, we do not abide with the particular plan. If even an eternity with God were to bring no peace, but only boredom and despair, then we might start inquiring as to what hell had to offer.

This happiness is not simply a feeling of pleasure or a string of pleasurable feelings. An everlasting sense of refreshment in a cold drink on a hot day would not amount to happiness. Happiness is more a soul pleasure which can almost savor a measure of pain along the way. Perhaps the word *peace* best describes the experience. The pleasure and peace of happiness are not the pleasure of a particular sense or the peace of a good, general anesthesia. Rather it's a matter of human wholeness. The person who is happy does not suffer from a divided spirit. Instead he experiences a directedness, a synchronization of his faculties, which stands in clear contrast to the states of despair, boredom, dissolution, and alienation.

The Bible and Human Nature

The biblical picture of an innate desire for happiness has two parts. The first concerns the generic nature of man; the second, God's promises. In Genesis 1:26, we find that God created man to be like God in certain unspecified but important ways. The Scripture implies here that man's similarity to God was not an interesting development or sidelight, but the very focus of the creative acts. And it is clear that the image of God was to be imposed upon mankind and not simply upon a select group of men. Whatever the particular image in creation, it is important to note that there was one image and not many conflicting ones. Despite man's diversity, there is a single Godlike thread running throughout the race. Similar treatment of man as a particular kind is found in Hebrews 2:5-8. Indeed the Bible is full of observations on the human condition, which presuppose a particular nature. The Book of Proverbs, for example, is full of prescriptions for all men. In Romans, human nature is discussed both in terms of conscience (Rom. 2:14-16) and passion (Rom. 1:26-27). And in these passages from Romans, we see that the fall has not erased the original nature of man, though man may foolishly and willfully violate his basic nature.

It is important for my overall case that there be a human nature, for it serves as the basis for all moral generalization. If men were randomly designed, then different things would help them and harm them. If, for example, some men found enduring peace in promiscuous homosexuality while others found it in sadistic violence, then the task of keying ethical rules to human needs would meet with frustration. If there were no common nature, then the various rules would simply encourage this or that faction. They would serve as formulas for satisfying the interests of certain segments of society. Rather than serving the deepest natures of men, they would violate the natures of many men.

Alternative Life-styles

Quite a few people consider the traditional values found in Scripture to be arbitrary. Talk of "valid alternative life-styles" often reveals a rejection of a universal set of human needs. As the account goes, certain people are basically homosexual or suited for sexual alliances outside of marriage. Their example serves to place a variety of new dishes on the smorgasbord of life-styles deserving consideration. Any attempt to remove this or that dish from the table is seen as imposing a tyranny of taste.

There is, of course, room for a wide variety of life-styles in Christendom. Zacchaeus did not have to adopt Simon Peter's snap decisiveness or his interest in fishing in order to become a Christian. Both the public life of Cornelius and the slavery of Onesimus were compatible with their Christian service. But there are lines which cannot be crossed, according to Scripture. Crossing them leads to ruin. The message is simply that there are universal ways in which men can confound themselves and others. Men are made a certain way and to ignore this is folly.

Although the Bible makes it clear that certain practices are harmful, it is not always clear what specific harm is involved. For example, is homosexuality harmful because it frustrates man's sexual well-being or because it undermines the family which is vital to man's well-being, or both? Does it primarily offend the conscience or destroy a social unit? Some commands seem to be simply aimed at hygiene (Deut. 23:12-13). Whatever the rationale, whether it be known to him or not, the father theorist accepts the command as grounded in a flawless wisdom concerning mankind.

God's Promises

Acknowledging the existence of human nature, we can go on to consider its specifics. One way to determine these is to see what a loving God promises those who follow him. These promises should reveal what he knows to be our fondest desires. If, for example, the Bible were full of guarantees of fame and wealth, then we might well conclude that God made us basically to itch for those things. Fame and wealth, of course, do not figure prominently in God's reward.

Consider these passages:

Blessed are the poor in spirit, for theirs is the kingdom of heaven (Matt. 5:3).

Have no anxiety about anything, but in everything by prayer and supplication with thanksgiving let your requests be made known to God. And the peace of God, which passes all understanding, will keep your hearts and your minds in Christ Jesus (Phil. 4:6-7).

Come to me, all who labor and are heavy laden, and I will give you rest. Take my yoke upon you, and learn from me; for I am gentle and lowly in heart, and you will find rest for your souls. For my yoke is easy, and my burden is light (Matt. 11:28-30).

> Happy is the man who listens to me [wisdom],
>   watching daily at my gates,
>   waiting beside my doors (Prov. 8:34).

Even youths shall faint and be weary,
    and young men shall fall exhausted;
but they who wait for the Lord shall renew their strength,
    they shall mount up with wings like eagles,
they shall run and not be weary,
    they shall walk and not faint (Isa. 40:30-31).

It seems that God, who knows us best, promises peace, blessedness, happiness, rest, and strength. Those are desires of mankind. We were made that way.

Cooperation with God

The obligist Kant would object to all this talk of reward for righteousness. For, on his account, you must distance yourself from an interest in happiness if you are to be truly moral. If you exhibit the least concern for what you get from an action, then your action lacks moral worth. Respect for universal law is the only genuine moral motive; all other concerns are mere incentives, carrots on the stick, if you will. But the biblical account is full of incentives, promised consequences. They find their way even into the Ten Commandments, "Honor your father and your mother, that your days may be long in the land which the Lord your God gives you" (Ex. 20:12). The list of gifts extends even to the material necessities of everyday life:

> But if God so clothes the grass of the field, which today is alive and tomorrow is thrown into the oven, will he not much more clothe you, O men of little faith? Therefore do not be anxious, saying, "What shall we eat?" or "What shall we drink?" or "What shall we wear?" For the Gentiles seek all these things; and your heavenly Father knows that you need them all. But seek first the kingdom and his righteousness, and all these things shall be yours as well (Matt. 6:30-33).

In thoroughly nonobligist fashion, God makes sure to mention the benefits of obedience to his commands. And in so doing he reveals that our interest in benefits is acceptable. Indeed that interest is part of God's design. He knows how we are made and proceeds accordingly. Interest in happiness then is not a less-than-moral interest, one which is at best irrelevant to righteousness. Instead, it is an integral part, consequence, or symptom of the righteous life. To will my own happiness and the happiness of others are not acts competing with God's will. Rather to will these states is to act in cooperation with God's will. To attempt otherwise would be unnatural and foolish. By promising us happiness, God has put his stamp of approval upon that interest. And to search for ethical guidelines which are insensitive to this interest is a contrived and curious practice. It is a striking example of throwing the baby out with the bath water. In an attempt to rid ethics of expediency and selfishness, the obligist often disparages that which is fundamentally important to us all. As we have seen, the consequentialist need not fall prey to the defects the obligist so disdains. The "father theorist," while a consequentialist, has room for all the hard-nosed honor or principle the obligist could want.

Cooperation with Nonbelievers

All this talk about God and biblical interpretation might seem to make what follows interesting only to believers. If you do not take the Bible as trustworthy, what room is there for interest in or support of an analysis of justice which focuses upon Scripture? How wide is the gulf between believers and nonbelievers on the particulars of justice?

The biblical response to this question is paradoxical. From one perspective, the difference is enormous while from another there are important similarities. The former notes the great difference between placing trust in God's directions and placing trust in the directions formulated by mankind. The opposing stances are those of humble submission and total self-reliance. Indeed, there is good reason to believe that this distinction is central in separating the kingdom of God from the kingdom of darkness. The issue is clearly one of authority.

Recognizing the difference, we look now to the similarities, the links. Since the nonbeliever is also fashioned in God's image, he has access to the same root conscience as the Christian. Both are disposed to reject certain practices as well as to approve others. Some situations strike both as abominable. If an account of justice is intuitively satisfying to the Christian, it is not at all surprising that his non-Christian friends will find similar satisfaction.

Shared intuitions do not, however, serve as the only grounds for common interest. If the biblical interpretation is correct, then it will serve the well-being of those who follow it. And this well-being ought somehow to show up in the world. Persons who follow God's directions ought to be happier and governments sensitive to his principles ought to prosper. Laymen and scientists alike should be able to notice the connection between certain life-styles and consequent levels of well-being. For example, one need not be a student of Scripture to decide that selfish people are less happy than those who exhibit a concern for others. Similarly, secular consequentialists could well observe the unrest generated by oppressive and cruel governments.

The fit between happiness, conscience, and Scripture does more than facilitate cooperation with nonbelievers. It also serves the Christian in his understanding of Scripture. Assuming both the love of God and the existence of a God-given conscience, he should be wary of readings which seem abominable or destructive. He should, of course, check the interpretation against other Scripture, and even be willing to accept a rule without really knowing the rationale for it. There must be a certain amount of trust. And when the admonition is clear, he accepts it as correct But when there is room for interpretation, he should feel free to use all sources of understanding to determine the correct one. To insist that an interpretation be reasonable is simply to respect our God-given rationality. In sum, a Christian account of justice is not provincial if it is correct.

Justice, a Part of Goodness

To summarize, we all seek happiness, and God, our loving father, directs us to it. His instructions apply to all of us since we have a shared nature.

We should remember that the justice we shall consider is not the whole of righteousness. It is only the righteousness of nations. Many of God's instructions will not be suitable for state policy, and so they will not appear in the account. While prayerful fasting and a spirit of forgiveness are important to the life of righteousness, they are not the stuff of civil law. And since just public policy is not the whole of virtue, this policy will not ensure the happiness of the citizens. The citizens of a just state may be individually miserable. Still, we may be certain that either the pursuit or achievement of public justice is in our best interest; for otherwise a loving father would not have urged it. Whether or not public justice is sufficient or even necessary for personal happiness, we may surely regard it as an ally.

Perhaps the practice of justice gives the society the analogue of personal happiness, a sort of social happiness. It would be characterized by internal cooperation, a basic organic unity and directedness, which fosters in its citizens a fellow feeling and mutual regard for peace and growth.

2
Desert

In the preceding chapter, one concept, father, served as the key to understanding morality. I hope to treat justice adequately with the same conceptual economy. For it seems to me that the notion of desert or retribution has the range and power to handle the matter.

The Common View of Retribution

Ordinarily, retribution is understood as only a part of justice; distributive justice, for example, is taken to extend beyond matters of retribution to the proper allocation of the benefits within a society; compensatory justice attempts to rectify abuses to citizens. The usual sense of retribution is limited to punishment. The very word has an unmerciful, ominous ring to it. Retributivists are often seen as tough opponents of prisoner rehabilitation and supporters of that chilling institution *lex talionis*, the retaliative principle which calls for "an eye for an eye and a tooth for a tooth." Even if these dreary associations could be ended with arguments describing the benefits and dignity of retributive punishment, the concept would still seem limited. After all, what does punishment have to do with welfare legislation and zoning laws? It is my task to make it clear how all these matters can be handled from the standpoint of the concept of retribution, and to show how this account honors Scripture.

In the process, neither Testament of the Bible may be ignored, for both reveal the will of God. If you dwell on the stern punishments of the Old Testament while ignoring the love directives of the New Testament, then you have a truncated account. If you focus simply on the warmer account of the New Testament while ignoring the sterner rulings of the Old, then you run the risk of treating the God of the Old as if he were radically different from the God in Jesus. If God is love and if he is the same yesterday, today, and tomorrow, then there must be some loving base even to the most uncompromising Old Testament account.

A Brief Sketch of the Theory

I give, first, a very brief sketch of the theory. If a person begins his search for a concept underlying a biblical account of justice by reading the books of Law, it is quite likely that his first candidate will be retribution. Those books prescribe punishments for a variety of sins. There is frequent reference to sin and guilt and their consequent judgment. Those words typically used to define retribution, merit, and desert, fit well with the Old Testament scheme. Those who transgress the Law deserve their punishment. So, there is a clear-cut category of *deserved harm*.

It is not difficult to extend the principle of desert to benefit as well as harm. A variety of passages tell us that those who work for us have a reward coming. A man's wage, it seems, is not a gracious gift but simply what is due him. To deny this wage is a sin; so there is the second retributive category, *deserved benefit*.

Perhaps, then, we have the two basic categories for a biblical theory of justice. A just government would dispense deserved harm and ensure that those who owe benefits to others pay them. This would be a fairly lean system, relying primarily upon the courts and regulative agencies. It would seem to leave little room for a wide range of social legislation. This, of course, would please some people, those dismayed by the sums we spend on different sorts of aid to the disadvantaged. Some speak derisively of the United States as a welfare state where a person is surrounded by care from the cradle to the grave. The two categories we have so far allow only for a person's getting what he deserves for doing something, whether good or evil. There is no room, yet, for giving people something for nothing.

But even a superficial reading of the Old Testament shows that deserved harm and deserved benefit do not exhaust the interests of public policymakers. For there is repeated reference to the plight of the poor and the oppressed. You expect to find the New Testament loaded with commands to care for the poor, but that kind of directive is not limited to the New Testament. The concept of victim runs throughout the Bible, but what do victims have to do with desert? If I am out of work because I was paralyzed in an automobile accident, what have I done to deserve help? I'm incapable of doing much of anything at all. If we say that I deserve care simply by virtue of my humanity, then we depart from the way we have been using the word *desert*. With wages and punishment, desert concerns the consequences of actions, not of inaction. If anything, inaction seems to deserve neglect. Does it follow that the paralyzed deserve neglect? The Bible seems to say that they should be helped, so perhaps the concept of desert has run its course without having reached all matters of public policy.

There is, though, a whole range of issues which can be touched without leaving the notion of desert. In order that it make sense to speak of something's being deserved, there must be a way for something to be undeserved. Complementing the broad category of the deserved is the even broader category of the undeserved. Applying the concepts *harm* and *benefit* to the realm of the undeserved, we have undeserved harm and undeserved benefit. It is my thesis that all matters of public policy, all issues of justice, can be handled within this four-part framework: *deserved harm, deserved benefit, undeserved harm,* and *undeserved benefit*.

All victims fall within the category of those receiving undeserved harm. Although they have not necessarily done anything to deserve help, an unsatisfactory situation exists if they are not helped. They have been harmed without having performed those acts which warrant harm. The Bible seems to say that this is an unacceptable state of affairs.

What, finally, of undeserved benefit? Is it also unacceptable? Apparently not, since the benefits given victims are undeserved. Indeed, these benefits are not only permissible, but obligatory.

The structure of the theory can be portrayed by means of a simple diagram:

	Harm	**Benefit**
Deserved		
Undeserved		

My task for the remainder of this work is to validate, unpack, and relate the four categories.

Rules and Desert

The concepts, desert, harm, and benefit figure strongly in this scheme and need to be given some attention. Since retribution is the central concept in the theory, I will discuss desert first.

There is a threat of circularity when desert is used to explain justice—"What is justice?" "Getting what you deserve." "What do you deserve?" "What justice demands." "But what does justice demand?" The task is, then, to break the circle, to give a separate account of deserving.

For the obligist, desert is a fairly fundamental concept. Along with right and duty, it lies close to the heart of ethical matters. Whether these notions are immediately known and valid or whether they are entailed by the more fundamental nature of freedom or ethical reasoning, they are quite basic. They appear early in the obligist program.

The consequentialist arrives at desert by a more circuitous route. His basic notions are happiness, well-being, and peace. He must work from them to an account of desert, duty, and right. If desert does not honor or serve human well-being, then so much the worse for desert. If it is to have any validity for moral choice, then it must be rooted in the more basic concerns of human happiness. In short, for the consequentialist, desert is more derivative than fundamental.

The father theorist believes that a loving Father, God, prescribes certain patterns of behavior for the sake of his children. The patterns are captured in rules, such as the one against murder. Now it is possible to regard each of these rules separately and to carry around a sort of laundry list of do's and don'ts. But this is impractical, unhelpful, and blind. First, it is blind because it ignores the natural groupings suggested by the rules. Second, it is impractical because of the strain the list puts on the memory. Third, it is unhelpful because it fails to provide a way to tackle new cases untouched by the standing rules, so summary principles and concepts emerge. They serve as a sort of shorthand for the rules, which are themselves specifically directed toward human well-being.

Desert claims are no more or less than applications of a working concept which summarizes a whole body of beneficent rules. The rules are roughly summarized thus: Respond in kind to harmful acts and beneficial acts and restore the loss to those who have been harmed without themselves harming others. These generalizations contain no reference to desert, reward, obligation, or duty. Instead they simply show the patterns which those in charge of administering justice follow if they do their job. They are not, however, mere resolutions or suggestions. A loving God does not burden us with trivialities or superfluities. Each rule has life worth and ultimately coercive sanctions. Whether in the form of the sting of conscience, the loss of institutions of value, peer disapproval, or the direct force of an angry God, the rules have weight. The concept of desert serves both as a handy way to do our moral bookkeeping and as a reflection of the force of conscience within us. It is a word of strong sentiment. When the passions cool, there is a calm, but forceful voice which speaks of desert and undesert. In sum, to speak of desert is not to transcend the human condition for it is simply a way of speaking of the necessities of the human condition.

God and the Rules

There is no requirement that God use the notion of desert in his own judgments. It is enough that he instructs and shapes us to use it. By virtue of his knowledge alone, he may ignore the rules we must follow. It is clear that in many cases we are to do as he says and not as he does. While God allowed Satan to torture Job to try his faith, Christians are not free to let their brothers suffer if they can prevent it. A father need not obey the rule he gives his child to cross the street only when accompanied by an adult. How much more may God transcend the rules he gives his children.

In some cases, God's acts offend our consciences or moral sensitivities. He has given us beneficent rules with consciences to help us in following them. There is a happy match between our most natural moral intuitions and our standing duties. But God's perspective is such that he may disregard both the rules he gave man and the sting of human conscience. Consider Deuteronomy 20:16-18 and 1 Chronicles 13:9-10. In the former passage, we see God to be unmerciful toward the inhabitants of Canaan because of their spiritual threat to the Israelites. Conscience surely demands that those who surrender not be killed. Yet God directs that the destruction be complete. In the latter passage we see Uzzah struck down dead for a simple act of care for the ark of the covenant. He made the mistake of touching the ark while trying to prevent its toppling over. Uzzah's death is as offensive to us as it was to David.

We can, of course, venture a consequentialist account in favor of God's action: God so earnestly willed the obedience and fear of his children, for their own sake, that he held Uzzah "strictly liable" for his violation. At that stage in the spiritual development of the Israelites, it was better to accept no excuses. They needed to be reminded of the uncompromising seriousness of God's plan.

Now whether or not this rationale is correct, there is still the fact that the deeds are shocking. But the shock should teach us that the rules and our consciences are provisional, that God's loving wisdom can transcend them.

Is God, then, just? If we mean by *just*, "worthy of highest moral praise," then he is just. He is a benevolent, not a malevolent, creator. But God isn't subservient to the rules he ordains for human public policy. He excuses things we may not excuse. He cuts corners we may not cut. He punishes harder than we may. He permits harms we may not countenance. In short, the children's rules do not bind the father.

Salubrious Retribution

In the final analysis, retribution does not generate rules for us; retribution itself is simply a family name for a group of behavior patterns prescribed by God. So, to say that someone deserves something is only to say that failure to give him that thing under these circumstances is bad policy for human well-being. The theory then is not so much an analysis of the notion of retribution as an ordering of God's commands using a word *desert*. The word has organizing power because of its grounding in human sentiment and the clarity of its bookkeeping image. When we use the word, we have images of debits and credits, of entries in plus and minus columns. We all know what it is to balance the books, pay the bills, and stay out of the red. The same sort of sensitivities are appropriate for our consideration of harms and benefits. God made us to think and feel in this manner.

When it comes to punishment, retributivists are usually regarded as tough customers, what with their demand that the criminal get his just deserts, what's coming to him. They seem to be retaliators, vengeful spirits demanding suffering. On the other hand those taking a rehabilitative position seem far more decent and caring people. After all, they want to help, not get even. Their concerns strike us as beneficent while the retributivist seems willfully insensitive to the matter of anyone's happiness. For them, it is simply beside the point here. What's done is done, and what's due is due.

The retributivism outlined in this work is, however, far from insensitive to human happiness. It professes to be both guided by it and most productive of it, given the human condition. Despite good intentions, loving acts can be bungled. Love is not always intelligent. The biblical retributivist's point is this: The punishment policy which makes for the most human well-being is retribution. If you care about your fellowman, you will see to it that those who willfully harm others suffer harm themselves. Other approaches to punishment go wrong. Honoring desert is a loving policy when properly understood. Desert is not a cold or inhuman concept.

Desert and Action

Desert arises when a person does something and not before. If I do you some good or harm, that act can create an obligation that I in turn receive certain treatment. That act of good or harm can either be one of omission or commission. Both rescuing a drowning man and refraining from rescuing a drowning man are actions, and can make me a deserving person. An infant cannot deserve at all since he is incapable of action in the full sense of the word. To say he deserves this or that punishment or reward is much the same as saying that a squirrel deserves something.

Small children are not punished for the sake of justice; justice does not demand that they be spanked. Neither do they deserve to be cared for, since they've done nothing for others. This is a shocking thing to say since no moral person would deny care to children. But the statement is not incompatible with child care. Children can receive care on grounds that the failure to do so would result in undeserved harm, an unacceptable occurrence. They are helped, not because they've earned it, but because they haven't earned the misfortune they face without help. So the objection is not to child welfare, but to conceptual confusion. You cannot play fast and loose with concepts without slipping into muddle and error.

There are, it should be noted, those who would question our deserving benefit. Some argue that as fallen creatures we deserve only to perish, that our own deeds are like filthy rags no matter how decent they seem. God, in his grace, rescues some from their destruction, but in no sense could they be said to deserve the good done them. Even the distinction between innocents and offenders is bogus, since there are no real innocents. What place then is there for deserved benefit? As with deserved harm, there is a body of biblical injunctions which can fill the category. Whether or not we ultimately deserve anything, God makes it clear that we should treat certain people as though they had something due them. The rule is that, when a person performs certain actions at your request, he is to receive a wage. If he does not work, then there is no need to pay him. The former we call deserving, the latter undeserving. At least for purposes of our social policy on earth, we are to employ the category of deserved benefit. It serves to distinguish the moral status of workmen from the moral status of vagrants. And, though perhaps ultimately there are no victims—no recipients of undeserved harm—we are instructed to act as though there were. The concept of desert here draws the vital distinction, for our moral decision-making, between Hitler and an infant. Original sin or not, they are to be treated differently.

Desert and Qualification

Although desert is a kind of qualification, not all instances of qualification are instances of desert. When someone murders another, he qualifies for punishment; he deserves it. So, too, is my qualification for my wage a form of desert. But when the victim qualifies for help, he does not really deserve the help. It is just that he does not deserve the harm.

Sometimes we talk as though all instances of qualification were matters of desert. We translate "qualified for the job" into "deserved the job." We speak of "many deserving applicants for the position," when we should say "many qualified applicants." This confusion arises primarily in connection with awards, grades, and positions with the corresponding expressions, "He deserved to win," "He deserved an A," and "He deserved to be president." This use of the word *desert* overlooks the important distinction between wages and grades. Wages are a return for service rendered. But this cannot be the case for grades. To think of an A as a reward and an F as a form of punishment is to construe the student as a beneficiary or victim. But are these students really servants or offenders? Obviously not.

In giving a grade, I simply claim that a student's competence and understanding lie at a certain level. It is purely a matter of description, not reward. He no more deserves an A than a ring deserves to be declared 18-karat gold. The ring simply is or is not of that quality and the assayer either judges it correctly, errs, or lies. The gravity of the error or lie depends upon what is said by the judgment. If by the grade I give you, I say your competency in philosophy is second rate, then my report can serve to keep you from qualifying for certain honors, awards, and positions. If my grade is correct, I have simply recorded the fact that you are less qualified than others. If it is incorrect, then I have harmed you unjustly. An incorrect low grade is in the same general family as libel if there is malicious intent. It's not that the person deserves the A; rather it's that he is A quality and denial of this can be harmful to him by selling him short.

The same analysis can be extended to other prizes and positions. In most cases, the harm is negligible. While with grades, the person may be placed clearly down in the pack, it is no great harm to be declared less than the most significant scientist in the world by the Nobel prize committee. Similarly, if I am not elected president of my organization, it does not follow that I am implicitly declared unqualified for the position. With or without malice, my nonelection could not qualify for libel because nothing bad is being said about me. Similarly, when I am denied a job sought by a group of applicants, I am not being insulted; for my qualifications may be impeccable. Since there is only a single job in this case, some perfectly qualified people may not be hired. Only if I am the single applicant for the job does the turndown run the risk of defamation. So discussion of awards, prizes, and grades does not fit in the category of deserved benefit, but in the category of undeserved harm. To say you deserve these things is to use desert in a misleading and confusing way.

Persons

Before moving on to a consideration of the concepts *harm* and *benefit*, it is essential to discuss the concept *person*. To understand how a thing can be harmed, you need to know the nature of the thing. What is harmful to soufflés may not be harmful to anvils.

Succinctly put, a person is a being which acts. To act is to behave according to your conscious choice. A choice is not a mere change of direction, but one made in light of a value system. When a computer selects one card from among thousands, it does not do so consciously. When rivers cut a new course, they move without a decision. When a venus flytrap grabs a fly, it weighs no alternatives. These three are simply not persons. The word *person* comes from the Latin word *persona* meaning the mask worn in a drama. The mask signified the character played. So the word has been tied to the notion of role, or mode of behavior. While this or that role determines which kind of person it is, the fact that there is a person at all depends upon whether it can play some kind of role. To be a person is to have a role-playing capacity.

The word *role* has come in for some criticism by association with the idea of false image or pretense. We are challenged to drop our masks, exposing the real inner person. But whatever roles we may play insincerely, we cannot drop all our roles. For to choose to drop all forms of selected, directed behavior would be a sort of personal suicide. No value system would focus our energies; we would become diffuse. In other words, the last mask is not a mask at all, but the face itself. Indeed, the masks are significant, too, in that they, rather than others, were selected. All masks present value facets of the person.

Action requires both an inner and outer life. Not all physical movements are actions. When a body heaves under electrical shock, that motion is not an action. On the other hand, sheer imagination without choice reveals no personhood. And choice without action is dead, to paraphrase James 2:17. The personality atrophies without behavior which accords with it. In fact, the behavior one exhibits may belie claims about this or that value system or choice. For example, if I say that I love someone, yet I exhibit great pleasure in criticizing him, then my behavior undermines my claim.

Personhood does not depend upon any particular kind of body or even a body at all, so long as the choices have some sort of effect in the world. For example, even if I am bound head to toe but able to perform psychokinesis, then I can act. So even if God has no body at all, he is a person since his will is capable of affecting anything there is and of creating things which are not. God needs no hands to move objects. But we, at least at this stage of the game, need bodies. Philippians 3:20-21, among other passages, gives us reason to believe our afterlife will be embodied too.

Are animals persons? There seems to be little reason to consider insects, fish, birds, and snakes as capable of action. For the vast majority of animals, behavior appears to be either instinctive or purely conditioned. Their behavior does not bear the mark of deliberate choice based upon a sorting of alternatives. There are, however, some chimpanzees who exhibit surprisingly humanlike behavior. They construct sentences by manipulating a machine, manifest a sense of humor, and seem to use a variety of ploys to achieve their aims. They can work on the level of a young child. Should they be treated as we treat young children? And are young children persons?

A Continuum

Rather than draw a hard line between persons and nonpersons, it would be fairer to construct a continuum of personhood. Some beings occupy a relatively fixed place on the scale; spiders are at the bottom end while a reflective adult is at the top. Somewhere in the middle we find chimps and small children. There is, however, a significant difference between the two in terms of potential. A child is potentially a complete person, while the chimp is not. Although there are similarities between chimps and children, the difference is significant enough to rule out infanticide and child-support payment for chimps. Although these two creatures may be close to each other on the continuum at present, the chimp is static while the infant is just passing through. Another obvious application of the "resident/traveler" distinction is to the issue of abortion. While the fetus resembles certain lower forms of life, it is a traveler and so warrants different treatment. This gives the fetus and the infant the same status.

Is the chimp a person? Not really. He does not seem to work self-consciously from a value system. From observing a chimp's behavior we may impute values to him. And there *is* a sense in which we can say that subhuman animals have values. The same thing goes for one-year-olds. But neither chimps nor infants can be called persons in the moral sense of that term. Still there is reason to treat a child as a sort of place holder for a person, since one will "arrive" there in a while. The chimp is holding a place for nobody.

Responsibility

Regardless of where one draws the line between persons and nonpersons, there are certain liabilities as well as privileges which go with personhood. To be regarded as a person is to be held responsible for one's actions. We do not hold chimps and children responsible for their behavior in the same way we hold adults responsible. Consider the absurdity or abomination of a murder trial for a chimp or two-year-old child. Of course, both are capable of killing someone, but we do not regard the killing as the act of a responsible person. Despite the fact that Ziggy killed his Brookfield Zoo trainer, he was allowed to live out his days unpunished.

The issue of responsibility is a difficult and sensitive one. How are we to treat fifteen-year-olds or psychopathic killers? Do we regard them as full-fledged murderers? On what grounds may they be excused from responsibility? Regarding the fifteen-year-old, it becomes a question of where on the developmental continuum we declare a human to be an accountable person. We have the choice of either setting a particular age of responsibility or of treating each case individually. In either case we would look for certain indicators of personhood. In the former, we might generalize on the age at which the indicators appear. In the latter we might examine each offender in much the same way we scrutinize those suspected of insanity. We would try to establish that there was a genuine choice made.

What might these indicators be? Following the lead of J. L. Austin, we might first look for excusing factors. If, for example, someone was sleepwalking when he committed the offense, we would regard his deed as one not strictly under his control. Similarly, if a man were hypnotized or slipped some drugs, he could be excused. If in *Mission Impossible* style he were deceived, he might be excused. If others make it reasonable to believe that a certain man is trying to kill me, I am not held fully responsible when I attack him. In each of these cases, the defendant does not know what's happening; he is not able to bring his values to bear on a situation. He either does not know the situation, or he does not have his critical resources at hand.

There is also a positive approach. It would involve observation and questioning to determine the presence of a value system from which the choice proceeded. Does he have a system of priorities upon which he acts? Is there a pattern in his behavior which would indicate a directed personality? Does the offender have a rationale for what he did? If the answer to these is yes, then there is good reason to describe him as a person.

Children and the Mentally Ill

If these indicators were followed strictly, then many six-year-olds and many of those we classify as mentally ill would be held responsible for their actions as persons. There is value in taking this hard line, though there is room for some mitigation. The six-year-old is more likely than the adult to have a faulty understanding of his act; he may not know that death is final, since the creatures blasted in cartoons spring back into action. He may have never had opportunity to consider an alternative set of values or the capacity to assess it. In light of the possibilities, it is appropriate for us to bend over backwards in withholding the charge of responsibility. But if it is clear that the child has rejected kindness and discipline and with hatred and full knowledge harmed someone, then he should be held responsible for his acts, for they are indeed acts.

Those suspected of mental illness are often excused, not for developmental reasons but for sickness. That is, their acts are regarded as so bizarre or abominable that no creature worthy of the name *person* could perform them. Those who behave so are often called sick or are compared to animals. Since they are regarded as less or other than persons, they are not held responsible. They are of course held in custody, at least for a while. Once they are judged to be persons again, they are often released.

The judgment that they are sick or beastlike is a curious one at times. Wanton violence is no more animal than it is human; indeed some argue that animals are incapable of the sorts of monstrosities man can perform. As for sickness, it doesn't seem to fit. When a person is physically sick, he suffers pain and damage. He is afflicted by a disease. But when a person is mentally ill, he, in a sense, is the disease. For the disease is often a collection of perspectives and values, as is the person. To be sure the perspectives and values are unhealthy, but this is nothing deserving special classification. Any value which runs counter to the teachings of God is unhealthy. The biblical name for counter-God values is wickedness. When this wickedness becomes so great that nonbelievers recognize it as such too, then it is often called sickness. And so much of what passes for mental illness is simply wickedness.

There is, though, some room for the concept of mental illness and for excuse on those grounds. Whether understood literally or metaphorically, the word *possession* should serve to order our thinking here. Not only must there be a new and different person at work. He must have seized control. If this new value structure took effect in total defiance of the structure in place, if the former person was rudely displaced by the latter, then there is reason to excuse. If there was an uncontrollable rotation of personalities, if the original person was more victim of than host to the visitor, if there was no overarching value which accommodated the shift, then it is inappropriate to hold him responsible. You would likely punish an innocent person. But if the defendant accepted, provided for, or ignored the dangerous new personality, he should be held responsible for its acts. He is guilty either of negligence or as an accomplice.

Ascription

With all our talk of love, it does seem that there ought to be a place for compassion here. After all, some insanity is brought on by terrible childhood experiences. A child raised by cruel and unloving parents is more likely to become "mentally ill" than one raised in a supportive atmosphere. What fairness is there in punishing the one whose background has undermined his well-being? Perhaps we are even determined in our choices by our genetic makeup and our environment. Shouldn't we postpone holding people responsible for their acts until this issue is settled? We could be sending victims to prison and worse. Here it would be good to introduce a second fundamental aspect of responsibility, ascription. The indicators named above are used to describe the responsible person. Because the accused may lie about his thinking, act deceptively at the time of the crime, simply not remember what was going on in his mind, or even deceive himself because the truth is painful, it is often difficult to establish criminal intent; but this is a descriptive task, one of correctly reconstructing the state of mind. When it comes to the question of a person's upbringing, description gives way to ascription. The Bible does not make room from the excuse of an unfortunate childhood. The court is not required to describe the child's formative years. In establishing responsibility, you do not give a person's life story. Rather, you ascribe or attribute responsibility to him for his choices; you hold him responsible; you treat him as though he were responsible. Now, is this just so much brute expediency? Where is the sensitivity, the love?

To go back to the beginning, God is a loving father whose commands are for human well-being. His directions are clear: Those who harm others are to be punished. Nowhere does it say, "Punish them only if they had a fortunate upbringing." Instead, regardless of their upbringing, we are to hold them responsible if they choose to do wrong. If this were not the policy, if upbringing were an excuse, then virtually everyone could plead irresponsibility, and the entire criminal judicial system would collapse or become mired. The staff of court biographers would present prohibitive costs. Abused children could enjoy a behavioral *carte blanche*. Sentencing would be based upon life stories instead of crimes. The alternative to holding persons responsible for their choices is absurdity and anarchy. A loving father would not allow this. He knows it is in our best interests to adopt a policy of rejecting excuses of this sort. Some people charge biblical retributivists with an ignorance of or insensitivity to the nuances of character formation. After all, they meet explanations of a person's problems with a call for punishment. It sounds as though the retributivist never studied psychology or thinks that it's the work of the devil. Neither of these is true; the retributivist is simply following the directions of the God who knows and honors our psyches best. By punishing all willful offenders we announce to all potential offenders that their past will be no excuse, and we treat the offender with a measure of dignity not accorded wayward animals and rivers. Whatever the reasons, the policy of holding persons responsible for their actions is in our best interest since it is divinely ordained.

There is another setting in which responsibility is ascribed. In cases of negligence, the court does not try to establish that the person actually considered the right thing to do and then rejected it. The defendant might well have been oblivious to the right course of action. Yet the aim is not to describe his state of mind, but to describe the state of mind that a prudent man would have had in that situation. The charge then is not that the defendant actually thought this or that, but that he failed to think something he should have thought. They hold him responsible on the basis of his general capacities, but not, in this instance, on the basis of their willfully evil employment. For example, if a driver while day-dreaming hits a pedestrian, he is not excused because he didn't intend to hit the pedestrian. He is held responsible because he should have been paying attention. Responsibility then may be either a standard we meet in our actions or one to which we are held in our inaction. Both approaches have biblical bases. Both concern our capacity to make choices, to act. We can find ourselves in jeopardy both for the way we exercise that capacity and for our failure to exercise that capacity.

Harm and Benefit

Now that the concept of personhood is sketched, the concepts of harm and benefit fall readily into place. Since a person is a being who has the capacity to act, a harm is anything which reduces the capacity to act. And since action has both inner and outer aspects, both decision and behavior, the harm could touch either the inner or outer person, or both. A befuddling drug and imprisonment would, respectively, do internal and external harm.

We might well use the word *freedom* in place of "capacity to act." When someone steals my tennis racket, I am harmed in that I must commit fresh energy, time, and money to resecure my ability to play tennis. Those resources were previously available for other projects, which must now be set aside. My options are fewer, my freedom is diminished, and so I am harmed.

As the complement to harms, benefits maintain or increase freedom. The human body does not continue unattended in a state of freedom. If no food and shelter are provided, it will die, so losing freedom. So the resources which maintain the basics count as benefits. Efforts which newly establish or reestablish freedom are benefits as well.

There is a sense in which our world gets bigger as the range of our freedoms expands. Let's use the expression, *world size,* to denote that range.

When someone gives me a tennis racket, the resources I might have used to get one myself are intact. Where once I had the resources alone, I now have the resources plus the racket, so I enjoy a gain in world size.

My benefit, however, need not be so personal. With each new discovery, the world grows larger, and as I am granted freedom to pursue the new things, my world size increases. The more possibilities in the world, the more freedom. If, for example, someone invents hot-air ballooning, I have a new freedom. There is a new thing on the scene which I enjoy the freedom to pursue.

There is, of course, a corresponding sense of harm. As the world shrinks, as there are fewer possibilities, I am harmed. I still have the freedom to pursue everything, but there are fewer things. When the last passenger pigeon dies, my freedom to own one as a pet disappears. This constitutes a harm.

Freedom and Happiness

In the discussions that follow, the word *freedom* will often stand in for the longer expressions, personhood and role-playing capacity. Its ubiquity should not, however, give the impression that it is the end of all human action. If policies of bondage generate more happiness than policies of freedom, then bondage is our cause. But they do not. God, who loves and knows us best, directs us to honor freedom.

3
A Matrix

Deserved Harm

First, we will consider the category of deserved harm, for it is the one which comes most readily to mind when we speak of retribution. The most striking passages report the stern punishment prescribed for a variety of offenses. The twenty-first chapter of Exodus and the twentieth chapter of Leviticus, for example, tie the death penalty to a wide range of offenses—murder, kidnapping, cursing or striking one's parents, human sacrifice, adultery, homosexuality, bestiality, serving as a medium, and negligence resulting in another's death. Of course, not all offenses called for the death penalty; if a man stole and killed a sheep, he was required to give the owner four sheep in return (Ex. 22:1). Regardless of the particular penalty, it is clear that since early in his dealings with man, God has directed that certain deeds be answered with harm.

It seems that the severity of the punishment is tied to the seriousness of the offense. We see in Exodus 21:18-19 that an attack resulting in less than death did not warrant execution. Rather the offender was required only to pay for the man's medical care and loss of time. The twenty-second chapter of Exodus goes on to assess simple restitution, not execution, for such deeds as kindling a fire which spreads to and destroys grain. The same spirit of proportion is found in what has come to be called the *lex talionis,* the law of retaliation:

If any harm follows, then you shall give life for life, eye for eye, tooth for tooth, hand for hand, foot for foot, burn for burn, wound for wound, stripe for stripe (Ex. 21:23-24).

Besides supporting the principle of proportion, this passage could be interpreted as prescribing punishment in kind, that is the identical harm in return; but this won't do as a biblical principle since other passages name dissimilar punishments. In Exodus 21:17, for instance, we see that the child is to be executed for cursing his parents, not himself cursed. It doesn't take much thought to reduce this principle of identical penalty to absurdity. The thought of court-administered rape is abominable, and it's not at all clear how blasphemy would be handled. Exodus 20:23-24, then, simply expresses a principle of proportionality. The challenge is to translate one kind of harm into another. In Deuteronomy 24:16, a simple, yet vital point is made. A person is to be punished for his own crime and not for another's.

> The fathers shall not be put to death for the children, nor shall the children be put to death for the fathers; every man shall be put to death for his own sin.

Strictly speaking, it would be improper to call the harm given a father for his son's sin "punishment" unless the father were being blamed for the son's behavior on such grounds as negligence or cruelty. To be sure, the practice of executing parents for children's offenses could serve as a powerful stimulus for responsible parenting. But this policy is unacceptable.

Of course, there are passages in the Bible which seem to counter this claim. In Deuteronomy 21:1-9, we find cities making atonement for unsolved murders in nearby fields. And in Exodus 20:5-6, we read of the punishment of children for their parents' sins. However one might explain God's purpose or meaning in this latter case, it is not presented as a guideline for public policy formation. As for the former, an analogy might reveal its circumstantial status. In military boot camp, whole platoons and companies are often "punished" for the misdeeds of single soldiers. For example, a unit may be kept out late because one soldier has lost his weapon, or the whole group may be held back from weekend leave until the few sluggards finish cleaning their equipment. Such "unfair" practices are designed to foster group identity, teamwork, and a sense of common destiny; and so might have those Old Testament directives in question. These instances of "group responsibility" can best be seen as situational and instructive for the Israelites rather than enduringly pertinent for statesmen. The scriptural notion of personal responsibility is more durable.

Deuteronomy 25:1-3 is a very interesting passage in that it inserts a requirement for human dignity in the midst of a fairly stern punishment structure.

> If there is a dispute between men, and they come into court, and the judges decide between them, acquitting the innocent and condemning the guilty, then if the guilty man deserves to be beaten, the judge shall cause him to lie down and be beaten in his presence with a number of stripes in proportion to his offense. Forty stripes may be given him, but not more; lest, if one should go on to beat him with more stripes than these, your brother be degraded in your sight.

Of course, every punishment, particularly if public, is a shameful thing for him who suffers it. He is held in contempt by his peers. But there can come a point when the harm given him loses the character of punishment and becomes wanton abuse. Even execution can become so terrible as to allow the offender no dignity. A slow, torturous execution could reduce him to a wild, broken person. If punishment is not handled within guidelines and with dignity, then the administration of justice is itself a disgusting spectacle. God cautions against this. The passage also uses the language of desert, demonstrating it to be a biblical notion.

Proverbs 17:15 implies that punishment is not only permissible, but obligatory.

> He who justifies the wicked, and he who condemns the righteous, are both alike an abomination to the Lord.

A similar note is sounded in Psalm 82:2:

> How long will you judge unjustly
> And show partiality to the wicked?

Regardless of how gracious it may seem to excuse the misdeeds of others, it is not a good policy. This sort of misguided compassion undermines the purposes for which punishment was ordained.

Punishment and the New Testament

But doesn't all talk of punishment ignore the New Testament teachings on love and compassion? Frequently the Old Testament law is regarded as outdated, as superseded by a new set of directives. But there are, nested in the New Testament, bridge passages to the Old Testament law. Christ himself speaks in support of the law:

> But it is easier for heaven and earth to pass away, than for one dot of the law to become void (Luke 16:17).

> Think not that I have come to abolish the law and the prophets; I have come not to abolish them but to fulfill them. For truly, I say to you, till heaven and earth pass away, not an iota, not a dot, will pass from the law until all is accomplished (Matt. 5:17-18).

And, of course, there is the classic statement of governmental authority, including the authority to punish, found in Romans 13:

> But if you do wrong, be afraid, for he does not bear the sword in vain; he is the servant of God to execute his wrath on the wrongdoer (Rom. 13:4*b*).

There does seem to be some continuity between the Testaments on these matters. But no sooner do you settle upon the preservation of the punishment principle, than you come upon a passage like John 8:1-11. Although there is some question on the status of these verses since they are not found in the earliest manuscripts, it would be too facile to disregard them, for they have the ring of authenticity; Jesus appears to be thoroughly Christlike here. The woman in the passage was an adulteress, qualifying for execution under the Mosaic law. Yet Jesus turns away her accusers and does not himself condemn her. He simply tells her not to sin again. What then of the Law?

The weight of this passage depends upon how broadly it is read. If Christ's action is seen as broadly exemplary for public policy, then the punishment model is broken. If instead it is seen as a particular way to confound the devious and self-righteous Pharisees and to demonstrate unmistakably his underlying love, then the model can remain intact. The first reading works upon the belief that Christ introduced love in place of justice, as though the two principles are at odds with one another. But if God was a loving father at the time of the Mosaic law, then his early directives were no less motivated by love than his treatment of this woman. To regard God's stern rulings in the Old Testament as less loving than his words in the New Testament is to take a sappy view of responsible parenting. The same people who regard the old law as unloving know perfectly well that their own children need some chilling and painful moments for their well-being and the health of the family. It takes wisdom, of course, to get your timing down, when to punish and when to refrain from punishing. The timing is largely a matter of considering the consequences, what will be most helpful. There is no inconsistency in a loving parent spanking a child at one time while simply admonishing him at another.

The severity of God's punishment directives can then be understood in terms of timing. Because of the special threat posed by the Canaanites to the development of his revelation and work, God might have come down particularly hard on certain offenses common to the Canaanites. His orders could have served as stern measures to ward off an infection. Other commands perhaps served to unmistakably underscore the indispensability of the family. By firmly rejecting homosexuality, incest, and adultery, God honored the family unit. Perhaps this was to secure its teaching and support functions. Perhaps it was to ensure that we understood the metaphor of God the Father and his family. Whatever the reasons, a loving God made it clear that the family was inviolable. Still sensitive to timing, the same God saved the adulterous woman from harm. This does not mean that he regarded the practice of adultery as less destructive; rather, in this situation he knew it best to confront the accusers and the woman with that essential element of the Law—love—to which they were blind. He pulled the rug out from under them because they were perverting the spirit of the Law. As martinets or bloodless bureaucrats, they were a disgrace to the very rules they honored. Christ's action was similar to that of a parent toward a smug tattler. He refrained from punishing the defendant in order to confound his accusers. To interpret this act as a shift in policy from punishment to mere counsel would be folly. For in the next instance, that same parent could come down hard.

This reading of the passage pictures Christ as suspending the rules to teach some men a special lesson. But it might be construed yet otherwise. This could have signaled not the mere suspension but complete revocation of the death penalty for adultery. That stern measure, once instituted as a sort of wartime directive, had had its day. Now that he had come, now that the revelation in Christ was secure, that particular public policy was obsolete. It was indeed a matter of timing, and we may understand that the time of the death penalty for adultery had passed.

A Division of Labor

Justice and love are neither antithetical nor complementary. Justice is simply a way of manifesting love. Love gets no competition from genuine justice. Acts of justice are a subset of the larger set, acts of love. Granting all this, what are we as citizens and Christians to do? Do we support a policy of mercy or do we administer the *lex talionis?* What sort of timing should we follow? How harsh a punishment should we select from a scale whose end points are execution and mere reprimand?

To begin with, there does seem to be a division of labor with regard to punishment. Recall the passage from Romans 13 and consider this one from 1 Peter 2:13-14:

> Be subject for the Lord's sake to every human institution, whether it be to the emperor as supreme, or to governors as sent by him to punish those who do wrong and to praise those who do right.

But Matthew 5:38-39 stands in stark contrast:

> You have heard that it was said, "An eye for an eye and a tooth for a tooth." But I say to you, Do not resist one who is evil. But if anyone strikes you on the right cheek, turn to him the other also.

The words from the Sermon on the Mount repudiate retaliation. Yet governments supposedly practice retaliation by God's ordination. Is this a contradiction? Not if the words of the Sermon on the Mount are taken to apply to the lives of individual Christians and not to matters of public policy. The parent can give a different set of instructions to the children and to the baby-sitter. He tells the children not to argue and fight, to love one another, and to obey the sitter, for the sitter is selected to rule the house in the parent's stead. On the other hand, he gives the sitter liberty to spank the children or send them to their rooms, liberties the children do not have toward each other. If an older child is appointed the sitter one evening, then that child has new freedoms in the use of sanctions. It is strictly a matter of roles. The same goes for Christians. As private citizens and brethren, they are to forgive and suffer harm without retaliating. As public officials they are to exercise their authority to punish. A Christian judge "turns the other cheek when he is insulted during a church business meeting; the same judge levies a fine on one who insults him in court. The Christian *as* judge is required to take actions that he *as* citizen is prohibited from taking.

Mercy

As administrator of justice, what guidelines should the government follow in punishment? When, if ever, is mercy appropriate? First, mercy concerns more than relief from punishment; the term also denotes acts of charity toward the poor. This aspect will be treated presently under other categories, undeserved harm and undeserved benefit. As for the mercy associated with punishment, it seems to be conditional. Numbers 35 outlines the institution of the cities of refuge. They were to serve as a haven for those guilty of involuntary manslaughter instead of murder. Only if the killer showed no mercy himself in the intentional act of murder did he receive no mercy. If some mitigating factor can be established, then there are grounds for a measure of excuse. It is a mistake to grant mercy simply because the thought of punishing another makes one squeamish. Punishment of genuine culprits is not only permissible; it is obligatory. Recall Proverbs 17:15, which called those who justify the wicked an abomination to God. To think that mercy toward a clear criminal is an instance of love winning over justice is fundamental error, for the very institution of punishment is grounded in loving concern. If there are no mitigating factors in a case, then mercy simply is sentimental and arbitrary. If it is based upon love, it is confused love. Returning to the recent analogy, the baby-sitter who lets the children "get away with murder" does neither them nor the parents any good. If, though, there are mitigating factors, the government is not withholding deserved harm; there is simply less or no deserved harm to begin with.

The *Lex Talionis*

Assuming that punishment is due, how does the government determine its severity? Does timing figure in? I propose that we view the *lex talionis* (law of retaliation) as providing the basic structure for assessing punishment. There are, of course, some problems with its literal application, such as rape for rape. But the broader principle of equal harm, not identical harm, for harm is workable. There is repeated reference to the principle throughout the Old Testament (Ex. 21:24; Lev. 24:20; Deut. 19:21). And while Jesus declares it to be bad personal policy in Matthew 5:38-41, it does not follow that it is inappropriate for governments. This division of roles has already been discussed.

The *lex talionis* seems to be quite rigid, but this is something of an illusion. Of course, it is demanding in that it requires equal harm and obstinate in denying excessive punishment. But within this structure of equal harm, there is room for a good deal of jurisprudential wisdom. This is because harm is variable both in the deed and for the accused. What might be a simple offense in peacetime might be a considerable one during war. And what stymied a different generation of criminals might not faze present ones. Some men actually break the law in order to get back into prison. Through their years of confinement, they have come to prefer prison life to life on the outside. Sending them to prison is not the harm to them that it is to a first offender. For a man who has relied heavily upon his reputed integrity, a short sentence or small fine can be a devastating blow, while for another that judgment would be negligible. Neither whipping a masochist nor deporting an enemy agent seems to have the force of punishment. And on the side of the offense, desertion during a battle is more serious than desertion during training maneuvers. Public drunkenness by the secretary of state during sensitive negotiations is more harmful to a nation than the same drunken condition while on vacation. Shouting fire in a crowded theater deserves more punishment than shouting fire at a polo match.

In setting sentence, the responsible authorities should do their best to balance the scale in the spirit of the *lex talionis*. This could call for some imaginative work and research. If, for example, a professional athlete were to cruelly break the hands of a concert pianist, he might, in partial return, be barred from professional sports for life. It is even conceivably just that he be crippled in some way so that he, too, is denied the chance of doing for pleasure what he may no longer do professionally. This is stern stuff, but not entirely out of line with some of the biblical injunctions. Consider Leviticus 24:19-20:

> When a man causes a disfigurement in his neighbor, as he has done it shall be done to him, fracture for fracture, eye for eye, tooth for tooth; as he has disfigured a man, he shall be disfigured.

And instead of sending the armed robber who is homesick for prison back to jail, the official might bar him permanently from prison and then confiscate some of his property. If he must be imprisoned as a preventive measure, care should be taken that his prison life does not match his earlier happy experience. Of course, the entire matter of crime and punishment might be avoided by simply letting him live in prison, provided he pays some sort of rent. The state should also consider the amount of harm which accompanies simple publication of the crime. If the deed is generally abominable to the populace, then the culprit has in store for himself a good many unofficial sanctions. He will find it difficult to move in prestigious circles, to receive honors, to marry certain ladies, and to find certain jobs. By publicizing the name of the offender the state acts to limit his freedom just as surely as if he is fined or imprisoned. A perceptive court will take into account the harm to the defendant which follows from a guilty verdict alone. For example, the devastation Richard Nixon felt in his fall from power might have been so great as to make imprisonment superfluous. It is crushing for a man seeking a historical, glorious image to be shamed before an attentive nation; he knows that every American schoolchild will learn of his duplicity and disgrace. It is powerful punishment to have your offenses immortalized. If, on the other hand, a public figure practically prides himself on his image as a scoundrel or if a particular offense arouses little public disdain, peer sanctions should not figure prominently into sentencing. The court should, rather, rely upon state imposed sanctions. There are cases, too, where even the highest level of public contempt cannot serve to lessen the state punishment. A murderer who tortures children warrants both contempt and full official punishment. The court has the responsibility to weigh all these matters in sentencing. To do this it must be able to discern the actual harm done to the offender by its actions. Such is the spirit of the *lex talionis*.

One more thing should be said here about the *lex talionis*. As we saw earlier, there is an institutional aspect to personal harm. Even though only I have lost an eye to a mugger, other citizens are horrified and intimidated by my harm. They are less likely to walk the streets; their public confidence constricts. They suffer a small measure of harm. The experience of an evening walk in the park becomes less feasible. A paralysis of fear crimps their role-playing capacity. So perhaps more than an eye for an eye is due. The Scripture, however, has taken all this institutional harm into account. Apparently, as a standing policy, an eye for an eye will do. The proportional formula is simple and intuitive, and so serves us well. This does, of course, leave an opening for adjustments when the harm is demonstrably quite serious. If, for example, I put out a pilot's eye in flight, thereby adversely affecting his visual perception and endangering the passengers, more punishment is appropriate.

The Fool

Where does this leave those harms we may call self-regarding? The court should punish those which significantly affect others. But what about those which simply ruin the offender himself? Are these harms deserved or undeserved? The Bible has a name for this sort of self-ruinous person; he is called a fool:

A fool's mouth is his ruin,
and his lips are a snare to himself (Prov. 18:7).

Like a dog that returns to his vomit
is a fool that repeats his folly (Prov. 26:11).

The fool folds his hands, and eats his own flesh (Eccl. 4:5).

And every one who bears these words of mine and does not do them will
be like a foolish man who built his house upon the sand (Matt. 7:26).

On the one hand, the fool does not seem as culpable as the one
who assaults another. But on the other, the fool seems more
culpable than the poor soul who is struck by shrapnel from a
terrorist bomb. Which way should we go?

The category of negligence can serve to place the fool's harms
in the area of desert. The fool is indifferent to the health and well-
being of a person; this attitude results in the ruin of a person. In
this case, the person is himself. He either neglects to consider or
learn the effects of his actions, or he disregards what he knows.
His disabling gluttony matches the thoughtlessness of a
daydreaming driver. Both forms of behavior are dangerous and
avoidable. One may result in injury to the heart while the other
in an auto injury. Negligence behind the wheel warrants
punishment. It will not do to say that you didn't mean to hit the
pedestrian. You should have been careful, and now you must pay
the penalty for your neglect. Does the analogy mean that fat
persons should be fined or imprisoned? No. For there is a
marvelous administration of justice which occurs outside the
courts. My negligence toward myself results in injury to myself,
and so I deserve harm; but I am already harmed to the extent
demanded by the *lex talionis*. Similarly, if my negligent behavior
places me in a position of danger, I receive equal punishment for
my dangerous action; that is, I am in a dangerous position. Fools
give themselves what they deserve. The courts need not intervene

unless the fool's actions injure or endanger others. Since the fool's harm is deserved harm, there is no obligation to come to his rescue. Compassion could motivate some care, but duty does not demand it. The fool must not be placed along the innocent victims of floods, muggers, and hereditary disease. The fool's sufferings are deserved. Children, of course, are neither negligent nor foolish in this sense. They simply lack the capacity to be negligent, because negligence presupposes the capacity to be competent. They are too immature to be negligent, and they have not reached the age for society to hold them responsible for being sufficiently mature.

Happiness and the Fool

Before leaving this discussion of fools, we might reconsider the connection with happiness. Isn't there an uncomfortable fit between the claims of God's beneficence in the first chapter and the laissez-faire approach toward the miserable in this chapter? If God's commands serve human well-being, then how is it that this reading of God's principle of justice permits so much personal folly and ruin?

The answer lies in the limitations of justice. The principles of public policy formation suggested by Scripture do not exhaust the biblical guidelines for good living. Indeed, the bulk of scriptural direction is for the individual and not for government. Piety, stewardship of talents, devotion to calling, moderation, a loving demeanor, turning the other cheek—these are the sorts of things the abundant life requires. But these are not the demands of justice. The fruits of the Spirit do not translate into governmental program guides. The spiritual commands, "Be still, and know that I am God" (Ps. 46:10), "Have no anxiety about anything, but in everything by prayer and supplication" (Phil. 4:6), "Bless them which persecute you" (Rom. 12:14, KJV), "Love thy neighbour as thyself" (Matt. 19:19, KJV), and "Let your conversation be as it becometh the gospel of Christ" (Phil. 1:27, KJV) are indispensable to attainment of a peace "which passeth all understanding" (Phil. 4:7, KJV). In our respect for these, our happiness is perfected. Yet, this is not the stuff of law. Imagine a fine for failure to engage in regular intercessory prayer!

Since justice does not require those acts of personal piety necessary for full happiness, it is not sufficient for such peace. Neither is it necessary for joyful communion with God. We are all familiar with stories of faith and spiritual triumph under persecution. The early Christian church survived and even prospered in unfriendly, unjust, surroundings. Today, the spiritual strength of Russian Baptists puts to shame those of us in more just circumstances. Does justice then lead to happiness or frustrate it? Is there a genuine connection, or are justice and happiness independent of one another?

We can imagine an alternative framework for government action, one based upon the old saw: "There are no atheists in foxholes." Victims are permitted to languish or starve so that their desperate circumstances will drive them to spiritual commitments. Murderers are excused so that society will be sufficiently terrorized to seek God. Ne'er-do-wells are injected with debilitating chemicals to curtail their self-ruinous behavior. Employers are permitted to defraud their employees, so that the employees may learn strength through adversity. In this society, there are clear opportunities for spiritual growth as a result of public policy. So why isn't this the correct approach if happiness is the point of all this? Why don't these policies better reflect the will of a loving God?

It's not entirely clear why God prefers a different approach to policy formation. There is no doubt that adversity often breeds spiritual devotion, but, for one of several reasons, God does not give us a persecution mandate. We do not read, "Thou shalt steal those of thy neighbor's possessions which preoccupy him," or "Oppress the poor and needy when it seems that oppression will do their souls good." Instead, we are forbidden to steal and to murder; we are commanded to open our hands to the poor and needy. Why is this so?

To begin with, God himself oversees a sweeping program of suffering for the sake of spiritual growth. This is a hard saying, but one which finds extensive support in the literature of the problem of evil. Not only does he permit Satan to operate unjustly in the world; he also allows a variety of harms in shaping history to his will. Whether we focus upon the plight of Job or the "thorn" in Paul's "flesh," we realize the existence and validity of a divine economy of suffering. In most cases, we cannot guess the purpose in suffering; but we can be assured that all of it suits God's wise design. This is a fundamental and provocative point of faith; we shall leave it at that. It was raised in order to show that, whatever value there might be in permitting or initiating persecution, the task is not being neglected.

Despite the fact that men can be happy while persecuted and the fact that in the most just societies men can be miserable, persecution is not the optimal condition for the development of lasting personal peace. Again and again in the Bible God urges and promises social as well as personal peace. Consider, for example, the happy image found in Leviticus 26:3-6:

> If you walk in my statutes and observe my commandments and do them, then I will give you your rains in their season, and the land shall yield its increase, and the trees of the field shall yield their fruit. And your threshing shall last to the time of vintage, and the vintage shall last to the time for sowing; and you shall eat your bread to the full, and dwell in your land securely. And I will give peace in the land, and you shall lie down, and none shall make you afraid; and I will remove evil beasts from the land, and the sword shall not go through your land.

These are the conditions we and God desire. These are the ones in which we are best able to "work out [our] own salvation" (Phil. 2:12). Here the family can prosper, the student of the Word can work unhindered, and fellowship and testimony can proceed without reprisal. Social peace permits the happy, fine adjustment of the soul, the free and forceful promulgation of the gospel. This setting is the fruit of just public policy.

It would be a mistake to ignore the other fruit of social peace, personal damnation. A person who is secure in his possessions, free from hunger and persecution, has the opportunity to reflect upon the condition of his soul, the order of his values, and the direction he shall choose in life. His choices may be wrong, his values upsetting, and his soul unhealthy. But it is important that there be a chance for a clear-cut ruinous choice. This, too, is part of God's plan. A just society, above all, seeks to preserve our freedom, our role-playing capacity; it provides for the freedom we need to save or ruin our souls. It preserves that important choice and so honors the will of a loving Father. God gives us this choice, and a just state preserves it. The conditions are optimal for the development of clear-cut saints and clear-cut fools. This is as he would have us proceed in setting the social stage.

But there is more to the connection between justice and happiness than this. For regardless of which conditions are optimal for the complete equipping of the happy believer, the pursuit of justice is important to that happiness. Whether the just state is the happiest state, the happiest people are those who work for the establishment of the just state. A loving Father, one who wishes and understands our well-being, directs us to do justice. Whatever the outcome of this project, whether we succeed or fail in establishing a fully just society, we may be confident that it is in our best interests to seek it. The happiness may come in the achievement of justice, in the pursuit of justice, or in both. Where it comes is not crucial. That it comes is as certain as God's love.

But how can we be happy when those we love are ruining themselves with state permission? Surely the spectacle of their self-harm is sufficiently grave to warrant a more intrusive government program. If justice is a form of applied love, if the principle of justice is salubrious, how can we say that justice allows people to be miserable fools? How can justice require us to permit drug abuse, for example? The same way it requires us to permit infatuation with material goods, obsession with eating, and indifference toward Scripture reading. The commandment, "Thou shalt not steal," requires us to refrain from taking away another's goods, even when the goods are sapping his spiritual strength. Imagine, for instance, that my new Corvette draws me away from my family, gives me illusory feelings of suave grandeur, takes money away from my children's cultural development, and stimulates me to wastefully burn gasoline. You would help me by stealing the car. As things now stand, I am a sad spectacle. And yet the commandment against stealing stands. It makes way for property freedom, an important component of personhood. How can a loving, just government permit the fool his folly? The same way it can permit the materialistic person his property. Both property and civil liberties can be misused. But a society in which folly and misuse of property are illegal is less happy and loving than one where these are permitted.

The key to this paradoxical affair—of happiness through legalizing misery—lies in the quality of happiness. It might well be the case that the purest and highest happiness comes from clear choices with obvious alternatives. When our right behavior is ensured by law, or when we are decent only through lack of imagination, then some of the luster of virtue is missing. There is a good deal to be said for the satisfaction which comes from spurning forceful, but pernicious, options in favor of righteousness. There is a fresh meaning to affirming life when first we understand the possibility of suicide. There is a higher sort of commitment, a greater freedom, a larger sense of personhood made possible by destructive options. And so the just state would make room for fools. As the state strictures fall away, our own corrective value structure is called into play, and we experience a new satisfaction and growth as persons in self-constraint. A state which makes little room for self-constraint is one which denies its citizens access to a higher sort of happiness. This is the point to the legalization of folly. And as I reflect upon this policy, I can find a peace which counters my distress at the fool's plight.

Victims

Now for the second broad category, undeserved harm:

	H	**B**
D	**Offenders** **Fools**	
U		

The Mosaic law can appear quite fearsome with its array of punishments, but nested among these is a variety of commands to care for others:

And if your brother becomes poor, and cannot maintain himself with you, you shall maintain him; as a stranger and a sojourner he shall live with you (Lev. 25:35).

For the poor will never cease out of the land; therefore I command you, You shall open wide your hand to your brother, to the needy and to the poor, in the land (Deut. 15:11).

When you reap the harvest of your land, you shall not reap your field to its very border, neither shall you gather the gleanings after your harvest. And you shall not strip your vineyard bare, neither shall you gather the fallen grapes of your vineyard; you shall leave them for the poor and for the sojourner: I am the Lord your God (Lev. 19:9-10).

The same theme is sounded throughout the Old Testament:

He who closes his ear to the cry of the poor
will himself cry out and not be heard (Prov. 21:13).

Is not this the fast that I choose:
  to loose the bonds of wickedness,
  to undo the thongs of the yoke,
to let the oppressed go free,
  and to break every yoke?
Is it not to share your bread with the hungry,
  and bring the homeless poor into your house;
when you see the naked, to cover him,
  and not to hide yourself from your own flesh? (Isa. 58:6-7).

While the Bible does show concern, repeatedly, for the poor, there are verses that recognize deserved poverty:

For even when we were with you, we gave you this command: If anyone will not work, let him not eat. For we hear that some of you are living in idleness, mere busybodies, not doing any work (2 Thess. 3:10-11).

A little sleep, a little slumber,
  a little folding of the hands to rest,
and poverty will come upon you like a vagabond,
  and want like an armed man (Prov. 6:10-11).

Their plight is the result of their own choices and so is deserved. They fail to act in a way which brings life-sustaining benefit, and so they fall into an unhappy state. But the admonitions to help the poor indicate that some poverty is not deserved. Some poor people are properly classed as victims not of their own laziness or folly but of circumstances beyond their control. Droughts, theft, disease, and floods can all serve to make you poor without your efforts. If it is to make sense to say a murderer deserves the harm he receives, there must be some sense in which you can receive harm you do not deserve. The notion of desert needs contrast if it is to have any value at all. The concept, victim, provides just that contrast.

The biblical account seems to say that these victims ought not be left without aid. Even when they do no work for the farmer, they are to receive some fruit from his field. This inescapable principle of helping unfortunates leaves no room for social theories which grant people only those things they earn. There are some who have no way to earn a living. They must be helped.

Public and Private Sectors

The help prescribed in the Old Testament was not strictly a private matter involving gleanings and sporadic acts of charity. Deuteronomy 14:28-29 pictures a public procedure for care:

> At the end of every three years you shall bring forth all the tithe of your produce in the same year, and lay it up within your towns; and the Levite, because he has no portion or inheritance with you, and the sojourner, the fatherless, and the widow, who are within your towns, shall come and eat and be filled; that the Lord your God may bless you in all the work of your hands that you do.

It might be argued, though, that this instruction was intended for the church of that day, so to speak, and that it is applicable only to today's church. In other words, it is a matter of concern for the private sector, and not the public sector. Charity is the church's business. But this reveals a misunderstanding of the public/ private distinction. These terms do not name absolute, exclusive, fixed kingdoms. This is not to say that the state should administer everything; it is not obliged to prescribe the number of times a week married persons are to express love for each other. Instead, it means that whatever men do there is potential public effect and that makes it the state's business. The state may and should grant large areas of discretion to its citizens, but we must remember that those areas are granted by virtue of their relative harmlessness and not with regard to some sort of absolutely private kingdom.

Regardless of how inviolable freedom of religion might seem, let one Moloch sacrifice occur and the police are on the way. And if transcendental meditation turns people into raving threats to community safety, it will fall under controls. No area of human activity is totally beyond review and control because no sort of human activity is totally insular. Officials may and should give the citizens and their organizations leeway to perform many of the functions essential to a society. Most people in our society believe that child raising is best handled by families. But when parents neglect their children, government intervention is permissible.

The baby-sitter, as it were, has the proper power of review over what the children do. If they naturally do all the right things, then he may sit back and relax. But if they neglect to do what is right, he must step in. He has been given the authority to punish, but he also has the responsibility to oversee the welfare of the children. If a child is hurt, he must be doctored. If the other children do not help the injured child, the sitter must see to it that the aid is given. He may give it himself or draft the other children to help him. Regardless of who does it, the sitter is responsible for that care.

The matrix of desert used throughout this chapter outlines the sitter's responsibilities. One of these is to address undeserved harm. If the citizens do not care for the poor and sick, then the state must step in and do the job. In our own situation, citizen care for suffering peers would only be partial, and so there is justification for state programs of care. Attention to unfortunates is no less important to us than it was to the Israelites. A loving God's instructions to them would serve us just as well.

The baby-sitter analogy is flawed in that the concept connotes the care of small children. The state, as baby-sitter, however, is responsible for overseeing adults as well as children, but we are granted a range of freedoms the ordinary baby-sitter wouldn't consider. Children are prevented from harming themselves, for example, yet the biblical account allows for people to be self-stultifying fools. Imagine, then, that the sitter is in charge of some mature children, and that the father, concerned that his children learn to make responsible decisions, instructs the sitter to leave the children to their injurious folly as long as the other children are not threatened. He loves his children intelligently. He understands that there must come a time when they are permitted to suffer from their unfortunate choices. In short, he treats them as persons and instructs the sitter to do the same.

Deserved Benefit

Now for the third category, deserved benefit:

	H	B
D	**Offenders Fools**	
U	**Victims**	

The wage theme is quite clear in Scripture:

> You shall not oppress your neighbor or rob him. The wages of a hired servant shall not remain with you all night until the morning (Lev. 19:13).

> You shall not muzzle an ox when it treads out the grain (Deut. 25:4).

> > Do not withhold good from those to whom it is due,
> > when it is in your power to do it (Prov. 3:27).

> > Woe to him who builds his house by unrighteousness,
> > and his upper rooms by injustice;
> > who makes his neighbor serve him for nothing,
> > and does not give him his wages (Jer. 22:13).

> And remain in the same house, eating and drinking what they provide, for the laborer deserves his wages (Luke 10:7).

Now to one who works, his wages are not reckoned as a gift but as his due (Rom. 4:4).

Behold, the wages of the laborers who mowed your fields, which you kept back by fraud, cry out; and the cries of the harvesters have reached the ears of the Lord of hosts (Jas. 5:4).

The concept of the wage seems obvious enough, but there are those who claim that, in our depravity, we actually deserve nothing but punishment and grief. Every good thing we get, spiritual or physical, is a matter of grace. But this view simply does not honor the passages just cited. Whatever our ultimate spiritual condition, our work on earth warrants pay.

Just Wage

These verses do not say what constitutes a just wage; they simply say that to deny a wage is unjust. But we are not completely adrift on this issue since we have already considered another form of desert, deserved harm. The *lex talionis* served as the core principle in determining the amount of harm due an offender. Can an analogue of that principle work for determining the amount of deserved benefit? How would it go? How might I benefit to the same extent that I am a benefit? To get at these questions, it would be useful to consider a wage-paying institution as an organism. A wide variety of organs are essential to the well-being and effectiveness of the body. Although the brain has a marvelous role to play in the organism, its effectiveness can be seriously checked by a torn fingernail. The pain can present a significant distraction, and the damage can simply rule out certain activities. And the absence of fingernails would present serious limitations to the body. Fingernails are not luxuries for the organism.

And so it is with persons. The chief executive officer, the records keepers, the craftsmen, the maintenance crew are all essential to the organism. Some like to point out that the executive officers can be absent for several days without anyone's noticing, but the janitor's absence is evident almost at once. This is not really a good argument for the superiority of janitors, but it does underscore their importance. The wage version of the *lex talionis* could well take the form, essentials are to receive the essentials. Or to put it another way, those who sustain life are to be themselves sustained. If I am an essential part of the organization, then for my contribution, the organization provides me what I need to prosper. The same sort of thing occurs in the organism; the healthy body supplies its various organs with the nutrients, protection, and other services it needs. Here, of course, the body is not interested in justice but in health and survival. Yet, since justice is, at base, a matter of well-being, the same sort of point could be made concerning institutions. Their health depends upon the state of their vital organs. Regardless of the specific threat to institutional well-being, the intuitive point stands—essentials ought to receive the essentials. It is quite reasonable to say that the organization owes full support to those whose contribution is indispensable.

As explained, this is an institutional principle. Although the work of the engineer at the water purification plant is essential to me, I don't personally owe him the essentials of life. He works for the city, and so the city owes him the essentials. The same thing goes for the body. Although the liver is vitally important to the heart, the liver does not bear the responsibility of providing the heart all that it needs; it simply does its part directly or indirectly to sustain the operation of the heart. Although you are now alive because your kidneys functioned a year ago, you "owe" them nothing if they do not function for you now. Although they saved your life by their work a year ago—if they do not work for you at present, their upkeep is none of your business. They may be removed or atrophy so far as the body is concerned. This applies even for the adrenals which act only sporadically. Only if they maintain themselves in a state of readiness for your personal use at a moment's notice do they earn their full keep. Even if adrenals and professional firemen are called upon only once a year, they contribute sufficient effort in terms of preparation and vigilance to warrant support.

A distinction should qualify this analogy, for it might be used to argue against welfare. The victim is not analogous to the dysfunctional kidney. His upkeep is our business. While it is true that he does not deserve his care, we must look to his needs lest he deteriorate undeservedly. It is, instead, the person who chooses not to work who is none of our business. So far as public policy is concerned, he may atrophy.

Stewards

There is another sort of deserved benefit not yet mentioned. It corresponds to the kind of deserved harm fools suffer. Just as a person can take certain steps to diminish his world, he can act to enlarge it. By exercise, careful eating, prayer, sensible use of time, prudent investment, and a great number of other practices, he can sharpen his faculties, lengthen his life, and increase his options. This gives him access to a larger world, so to speak. These benefits are deserved in a way that those based upon, say, heredity are not. They may diminish or increase according to life-style. The person who cultivates his God-given powers is wise. The Book of Proverbs describes him as it does his counterpart, the fool.

	H	B
D	**Offenders Fools**	**Servants Stewards**
U	**Victims**	

Undeserved Benefit

In considering the category, undeserved harm, we saw that there are occasions when undeserved benefit is not only permissible, but obligatory. Victims must be given assistance even though they've done nothing to deserve it. This is not, of course, to say that they are contemptible. Their undeserving condition is not a matter of moral failure. Indeed, they lack the capacity to be guilty of the pertinent moral failure, sloth. For one reason or another, their capacity to perform, whether admirably or culpably, is depleted, and we must protect and rejuvenate them. So, strictly speaking and through no fault of their own, the help we give is undeserved. There are, then, in a just state, beneficiaries.

If undeserved benefit is a worthy state policy, then why stop at helping victims? Why not extend our assistance to fools? A man who ruins himself by means of drink, prodigality, or inattention to hygiene could stand some help. His role-playing capacity is below par. What is to prevent us from restoring his basics? Very simply, we would be undermining his freedom, his freedom to be a fool. If we catch him whenever he falls, then it becomes difficult for him to effectively ruin himself. For reasons given earlier in this chapter, this would be a mistaken policy. We would, so to speak, be guilty of obstructing justice. He's earned his harm, and now we act to prevent it. In attempting to secure a society in which one cannot lose, we all lose a basic freedom.

Victims, though, are not the only proper beneficiaries in a just society. We all are. The following passage points the way:

And God blessed them, and God said to them, "Be fruitful and multiply, and fill the earth and subdue it; and have dominion over the fish of the sea and over the birds of the air and over every living thing that moves upon the earth" (Gen. 1:28).

Recall the comments on *world size* in the previous chapter (pp. 46-47). My freedom of access to everything can be increased by the addition of more things. The bigger the world, the greater my role-playing capacity. And so, by enlarging the world, the state makes every citizen a beneficiary. How does this happen, and what's the connection with Genesis 1:28?

As we fill and subdue the earth, we make more things available. Exploration, research, and engineering identify and secure for us new opportunities. Whether we chart the Northwest Territory, discover penicillin, reach the moon, harness the atom, develop hybrid corn, or build roads into Yellowstone, we present each other with new possibilities. All this activity fits Genesis 1:28 nicely. The earth is for our stewardly advantage, and it is both our privilege and task to make the most of it. The just and vital state accepts this task. The rationale may be that of defense against victimization. Both cancer research and space exploration can be construed as a form of defense. But the rationale may be more than defensive. For the positive aim of world enlargement is both honorable and desirable for the state.

The project of world enlargement must not be confused with international expansionism or environmental rape. Instead, it is the introduction of totally new entities. We do not justly enlarge our world by seizing Ethiopia, but by discovering the Grand Canyon. As for the environment, if we are ruthless or careless, we may well diminish our world rather than enlarge it. In our rush to add new things to our world, we must take care to maintain as many of those things we already enjoy as we can.

Wealth

Some might wonder what is to be said, in this context, for great wealth. If by our labor we deserve the essentials, what do we make of those goods we possess beyond the essentials? Aren't these undeserved benefits? Are they legitimate or unjust? Should we level all income, eliminating this sort of undeserved benefit, or should we encourage it?

The only state interest in this context is to provide the possibility for wealth. The state is not only concerned to make A a possibility for you, B a possibility for you, and C a possibility for you; there is yet another possibility it wants to maintain, the possibility that you personally enjoy A, B, and C. To put it otherwise, the state should try not only to make each thing a possibility for you, but also to make the enjoyment of many things a possibility for you. This possibility of wealth is a component of your basic freedom. Any attempt to rule out wealth per se would be a contrived limitation of freedom, a harm. Of course, wealth must not be permitted at the expense of others' basic freedoms.

This completes the matrix:

	H	B
D	**Offenders Fools**	**Servants Stewards**
U	**Victims**	**Beneficiaries**

The Lesser Evil

The matrix provides an outline of the principles which compose the concept of justice. Among these are "Do not harm innocents," "Punish offenders," "Help victims," and "Reward responsible workers." It is commonly thought that principles such as these are sometimes so inextricably bound in conflict that people are forced to violate one or the other. These frustrating conflicts are called moral dilemmas. One of the classic dilemmas concerns an overloaded lifeboat. If several innocent passengers are not cast overboard, then the lifeboat will sink, killing all the passengers. It seems that some must die undeservedly in order that others not die undeservedly. Since justice demands that innocents not be killed, we have a situation in which an injustice is performed in the interest of avoiding other injustices. Here is the practice of victimizing some to prevent the victimization of others. The familiar expression to cover this choice is "the lesser of two evils." It is understood that this is a morally messy world in which absolute allegiance to any rule, such as "Don't harm innocents," is impossible or immoral. We simply have to compromise now and then.

Much of this reasoning is utilitarian and so consequentialist. You place the anticipated happiness and unhappiness on the pans and the tip of the scale indicates the moral choice. The innocent loss of life in Hiroshima, Nagasaki, and Tokyo is weighed against the unjust loss of life involved in the invasion of Japan and comes up short. And so the uranium, plutonium, and incendiary bombs are dropped. It's not a pleasant choice to make, but the alternative seems worse. But, as pointed out in the first chapter, utilitarianism has the fatal flaw of arrogance. Men, whose understanding is limited, make the calculations themselves. God, whose calculations are without error, is ignored. Since his directions are beneficent, it is, at best, odd to contravene them in the name of beneficence. It treats his commands as more platitudinous than perceptive.

Utilitarians are not the only ones who countenance a measure of injustice in the service of justice. The intuitionist W. D. Ross presents what could be termed a hierarchy of moral considerations. Our duty to protect human life is, for example, higher than our duty to respect property rights. Theft is permissible if it is necessary to save a life. Ross qualifies this, though, in terms of trailing obligations such as the obligation to try to repay the theft victim after the fact. This approach is clearly nonutilitarian, but it, too, involves a sort of lesser-of-two-evils thinking.

There are, I believe, several reasons for rejecting lesser-of-two-evils thinking. This is not to say that God avoids it himself or that there have been no occasions when it was appropriate. We have seen commands which reflect just such an approach; when the Israelites were told to kill everything in Ai, they faced the task of harming innocents such as the children. It was, however, essential to the formulation of Judaism and then Christianity that the influence of the Canaanites be struck down. This policy, because it was based upon a special command from God, does not alone entitle us to act similarly toward our enemies. It does not have the character of one of the Ten Commandments. Indeed, it is no part of the law at all. In the absence of similar special guidance, the rules stand. Though God may consider the lesser of two evils in his actions, it would be a mistake for us, with our flawed and always limited perspectives, to do so.

One reason might seem too facile to be significant or fair. It is simply that the Bible tells us not to do certain things, period. Exodus 20:15 reads, "You shall not steal." This is not a conditional command. And although Exodus 21 would seem to mitigate Exodus 20:13, "You shall not kill," it actually interprets the command. It compels us to read the command as a prohibition against killing innocents, against murder. And here it stops.

Perhaps this all seems like question begging, assuming the very inflexibility which is in question. But the unqualified form of the law does at least warrant our placing the burden of proof upon the situationalist. Since the commands came directly from God, anyone who wants to compromise them ought to have to explain himself in stunning fashion. He likely will call the Ten Commandments "general guidelines" which may become inapplicable in specific situations. They are meant to reveal the spirit of God's will, respect for life, property, the family, and so on. These are the beginning points, not the last word in moral deliberation.

This is certainly one way of reading God's commands, but I don't see that it is the best or most reasonable way. For it treats these commands as far less helpful than they might be. It's not really clear on this interpretation why God even bothered with the

Commandments at all. If, for example, our utilitarian calculations could override one of them, then why did he not simply command us to seek to maximize happiness in all our acts? And if our intuitions could serve to set aside specific commands, why did he not simply instruct us to follow the dictates of conscience? Doesn't the detailed instruction he gives us reveal a lack of trust in our capacity to sort out these matters for ourselves? And doesn't the perennial disagreement on ethical issues among men of the most cultivated conscience undermine the faith that a loving God would have left so much up to us? We need more than general direction; we need specific instructions. Our finitude and fallenness place us at a severe disadvantage in moral decision-making. Wouldn't it be more reasonable to suppose that a loving God supplied rules to solve dilemmas rather than generate them? More on this in a moment.

The Firing Squad Case

Let's focus upon the difficulties of utilitarian calculations. Consider the following case based upon one given by Bernard Williams in his *Utilitarianism*: An American scientist studying the wildlife of a South American country enters a village. There has just been a *coup d'etat*, and the new government is anxious to establish its authority throughout the nation. Posters antagonistic to the new regime have appeared in the village and troops have been sent to stifle the resistance. They have selected, at random, ten men to be executed. The technique is ruthless but, they believe, effective in teaching the watching village and nation a lesson—villages which harbor traitors will be punished. No trial is necessary to make the point. Deterrence, not justice, is at issue. The commander of the firing squad spies the American and has a brainstorm. If the American were to kill one of the men, it would symbolize the solidarity of the American people with the new government. He explains this to the scientist and offers to release the other nine men if he will cooperate. The families leap on the offer, begging the scientist to kill one of the men. This would reduce the chances of being killed for each man from 1:1 to 1:10. What is the scientist, a utilitarian, to do?

He sketches a number of scenarios:

(1) I kill the one, saving nine, thereby maximizing happiness.

(2) In killing the one, I lend symbolic support to the government, which, newly strengthened, goes on to kill other opponents with abandon, thereby undermining happiness.

(3) I turn the gun on the soldiers, thereby dying a martyr without saving the others, an unhappy situation.

(4) My martyr's death incenses the American government which intervenes to depose a murderous government, thereby maximizing happiness.

(5) My martyr's death and ensuing American intervention establish a big brother resentment in the hearts of the people resulting in an even more grievous revolution and regime in the future. Happiness loses.

(6) By shooting the one man, I support the government, which proves to be the most felicitous of the alternative forms of rule.

(7) I shoot the one and thereby give rise to moral outrage throughout the land, which precipitates a revolution ending the present government. This maximizes happiness.

(8) I allow the ten to be killed, thereby saving them the eventual anguish of death from disease which strikes a majority of these people. In their absence, the families learn a new toughness which enables them to meet life's trials more successfully and happily.

(9) I refuse to kill the man, thereby maintaining a sort of moral purity which is essential to my reputation as a spokesman for environmental concerns in America. Any loss of respect for me would hurt the environmental projects so vital to the well-being of mankind.

(10) I kill the man, enhancing my reputation as a morally sensitive and tough man. This makes me a more effective spokesman for environmental concerns tied to the happiness of mankind.

And so on and on the calculations can go. In any choice there is a devastating range of possible consequences. Is it not reasonable to suppose that a loving God would come to our aid with rules? For he has the power both to read and write the future.

Traditionally utilitarianism faces attempts to reduce it to absurdity. For example, a utilitarian might be compelled to break up a terrorist hijacking by murdering, one by one, the children of a terrorist. If the terrorists are clearly intent upon killing scores of passengers and if only the deaths of their children would dissuade them, then there is warrant for a display of child execution on the runway in sight of the plane. Of course, the utilitarian can try to wiggle out of this, and his opponent can tighten up the dilemma in return. The point stands that there is nothing in pure utilitarianism to rule out this sort of shocking choice. But the father theorist has the same problem. He, too, may be warranted in killing children, as he was at Ai. The advantage he has here is clear, though. Whereas the ordinary utilitarian faces the awful act with impartial data, the father theorist proceeds in this way only upon direct orders from God, who has all the data. Once the utilitarian assumes the freedom to depart from the Commandments, he also shoulders the responsibility for making the Ai-like calls himself. This is a horrible responsibility, particularly since it is one he is not competent to handle, given his finitude. Of course, the father theorist at Ai has the heavy responsibility of determining whether he has a genuine, special message from God.

The Brinks Case

As for the intuitionists, they are plagued by conflicting intuitions much as the utilitarians are plagued by conflicting scenarios. Thoughtful and sensitive men are at odds on a wide range of ethical issues. Even the standard life-over-property intuition can waver when confronted by a case such as the following Brinks Dilemma: A Brinks driver, who has delivered a million-dollar payroll to Kennedy Airport for years, falls under the conviction that he should help those starving to death in Somalia. Careful research tells him that he can probably subdue his partner, ditch the truck, board a plane for Switzerland, and deposit the money in a Swiss trust account, all without detection. Even if he is captured, the money will be missing, at work saving lives in Somalia. Checks pour from the trust, supporting one hundred lives indefinitely. Meanwhile back in the United States, Brinks' insurance company covers the loss, the airport employees are paid, insurance and Brinks rates rise slightly, and security is tightened. Nobody in the United States is seriously inconvenienced, much less killed.

So here is the trade-off: One hundred lives are saved by means of some inconvenience to others. This is a far cry from the life-*versus*-life decision facing the scientist in the South American jungle. In the present case, lives can be saved without taking life. Isn't then the lesser-of-two-evils theorist not only permitted but obliged to attempt the heist if there is reasonable hope of success?

The driver would rather use other means, but he knows he has no hope of raising a million dollars honestly. A confidant tries to argue against the robbery on grounds that the citizens of Somalia are, because of their alien status and distance from America, no concern of ours. But the driver finds this principle less intuitive than the original life-over-property principle.

Many, if not most people, cannot condone the driver's action even though it is based upon the life-over-property principle. Very simply, if he does not act, one hundred people will soon die. Yet we balk at helping them in this fashion. The means to the end seem unacceptable even though this is a life or death matter. The hierarchy of duties is jolted. Robin Hood doesn't come off so well when he robs honest people, even though lives are at stake.

Should not the Commandment, "You shall not steal" (Ex. 20:15), sit in judgment upon intuitions rather than intuitions pass judgment upon the Commandment? Doesn't Scripture validate the intuitions opposing the heist while invalidating those which support the driver?

Just Means

My position then is this: Neither utilitarian calculation nor intuition, both of which support lesser-of-two-evils thinking, is trustworthy. Neither has the epistemic weight to override a biblical prohibition. Neither can support an unjust act, even in the interest of justice. The desert matrix reveals both positive obligations and prohibitions, things to do and things not to do. We are to aid victims, punish offenders, and pay workers. We are not to harm innocents. The positive obligations focus upon the ends, the negative upon the means. We are told to undertake certain projects but to avoid particular methods. The obligation can simply be expressed, "Do justice justly." Help victims without victimizing. Punish offenders without punishing nonoffenders. Pay workers without penalizing others. The Bible leaves us great latitude in choosing techniques for the administration of justice. I may help the poor by means of cash payments, food stamps, interest-free loans, vocational guidance and training, and Thanksgiving baskets; but I may not help the poor by murdering rich people and seizing their goods for distribution, or by denying employees their wages. Again, the maxim is "Do justice justly." A corollary to this is the maxim, "Never victimize." And if the aims of justice cannot be met without doing injustice, then the aims of justice cannot be met. If we cannot punish offenders without intentionally harming others, then some offenders will simply have to go unpunished. Justice, yes, but not at all costs. The cost of unjust means is too high. It is "expensive" to disregard biblical prohibitions.

A Straw Man

Those who oppose lesser-of-two-evils thinking often encounter a straw man. The situationalists construct a life-or-death dilemma. When the nonsituationalist rules out the lifesaving injustice, the situationalist pictures him as a sanctimonious fellow, one who stands by and lets others die for the sake of preserving his moral purity. Preferring rules to people, he lets others suffer. He "fiddles while Rome burns." This is the straw man.

Returning to the South American firing squad dilemma, we see the situationalist ask rhetorically and incredulously, "You mean to say you'll just stand there and watch nine murders you could have stopped?" This question describes what the situationalist takes to be the only significant option to killing the one. But rhetorical question or not, the answer is no. All the nonsituationalist means is that he will not shoot the innocent man. He has a number of other options:

(1) Turn the rifle on the firing squad, hoping these heroics will serve to break up the execution.
(2) Pray earnestly for a miracle.
(3) Argue and plead for their release.
(4) Stand in front of the prisoners.
(5) Exhort the village to insurrection.
(6) Present an alternative plan to the firing squad.
(7) Attempt to buy the release of the men.

Certainly there are others, but the point should be clear. The choice is not between killing an innocent man and doing nothing. There is a variety of possible actions, some of which could involve personal loss of life. The nonsituationalist does not refuse to act with compassion; he refuses to do a particular thing, even with compassion.

Obviously the seven options listed above are long shots. It might seem wrong to choose an option whose probability of success is below that of the single killing. But this sort of calculation is the very sort the commands of God are intended to displace. The figuring has already been done for us. To press on here is to question God's math, so to speak.

Finitude

It is wrong to justify a victimizing act on the basis of lesser-of-two-evils thinking. But there is a context in which it is appropriate to consider the lesser evil. The battlefield practice of triage illustrates this point. At field hospitals, there is a tradition of sorting incoming wounded by the gravity of their injury. Those who will die despite attention are left alone. Those who will live without immediate attention are laid aside for a time. The third group, those whose lives are in the balance, become the focus of medical care. Now, of course, the modern field hospital is often suitably manned and marvelously equipped for prompt and effective attention to virtually all casualties. But the practice still has its day. There are times when the flood of wounded exceeds the staff's capacities, and choices must be made. In these cases, triage or something like it is necessary.

Let us imagine that the medical crew has all it can do to save the lives of a dozen soldiers suffering from massive head wounds. As they work, another soldier lies to the side with a very dirty puncture wound in the foot. As the desperate surgery continues, the infection spreads through the foot and lower leg. By the time they reach him, the damage is a good deal more extensive than it might have been had the wound been treated promptly. The soldier may lose his foot or be bound to a bed well past the armistice. He, in short, suffers harm, and if his cause is just, it is unjust harm. His loss of role-playing capacity is wrong, yet we must accept it in this context.

The simple reason for our inattention is finitude. There just seems to be more injustice than we can correct. And so we must choose which to address. We must decide which is the lesser evil. But this is not the same as making victims ourselves. The doctors themselves do not infect the soldier. The evil continues because they are unable to meet it. Of course, they might leave the operating tables and work on his foot, but then the others would die—more injustice. They try to meet the greater injustice, loss of life, rather than the less debilitating injustice of the foot wound.

The state, while attacking all the injustice it can, must realize that either at some time or at all times, there is more injustice than can be met. And so it must be prepared to make the same sort of choice the doctors made in the example above. And we must refrain from calling this choice unjust. While some may continue to suffer, it is not because of our malevolence, but our finitude.

Claims of finitude must not come cheaply or disingenuously. We must not use them to excuse acts of mere convenience or policies of indifference. But where the limitations are genuine, we should be as discriminating as those doctors.

Summary

This completes the structure of the theory. To recap, it rests upon the belief that the commands and deeds of God are those of a loving Father. We, his children, for our own well-being, should acknowledge his beneficence, omniscience, and omnipotence by strict obedience. These divine instructions fall within a matrix of desert. Its categories are deserved harm, undeserved harm, deserved benefit, and undeserved benefit. The matrix gives the state its job description as "baby-sitter." The rules for the children are somewhat different; that is, private citizens have a different role from state officials. In pursuing the goals of justice, the state is to avoid doing injustices. The state which observes these principles is blessed.

Equality

Before moving on to more detailed application of the theory, I should comment briefly on two concepts which figure prominently in several other theories, *rights* and *equality*.

In the interest of personal freedom, the just state maintains an entitlement structure which permits some citizens to amass wealth. And so pure equality of distribution is not its aim. But there is a sense in which equality plays an important role. Since the principles of justice apply to persons without discrimination, they provide equal treatment. All offending persons are treated as offenders. All victimized persons are treated as victims. In other words, all persons are equal before the law. This is the sort of equality the theory embraces.

Rights

What place does this theory leave for the concept of rights? Is it legitimate to speak of human rights? The answer is an unenthusiastic yes. While the rules can be translated into rights talk, rights talk can take on a life of its own which ill fits the rules. The rule, "Stop and correct the undeserved harm a child suffers," can be construed, "A child has a right to protection and care." "Don't steal" can be read, "There is a human right to property," and "Don't murder" reads, "There is a right to life." When President Carter spoke of the importance of securing human rights in the world, it was fitting to agree; for it is good to oppose undeserved harm.

Some identify rights with interests instead of basic needs, and this is fine up to a point. Say you're interested in collecting the autographs of film stars. The father theorist would rule out attempts to keep you from your hobby; for these interferences would constitute a loss of freedom, a harm, a limitation of your role-playing capacity. Of course, if you secure the autographs by kidnapping, you become an offender, and the interference you suffer is deserved. So the rules of the matrix both provide for and delineate the hobby. The rights version goes as follows: You have a right to collect the autographs. The stars have a right to move about as they choose. Their right is more fundamental than yours, and so, in kidnapping, there is a rights violation. The moral of the account is "Don't kidnap for autographs." This is obviously the same moral as the one based upon the matrix. So what's the problem?

The danger in talk of rights lies in its tendency to encourage lesser-of-two-evils thinking. Note the difference between the two approaches to the autograph-seeker problem. With the matrix, there is nothing at all evil in jailing or blocking the kidnapper. The rule supporting his hobby has not been suppressed, overridden, or superseded by the rule that the stars' freedom of movement must be preserved. Nothing morally valuable has been lost in denying him the freedom to kidnap, for his original freedoms are stated in terms of his innocence. The rule states that innocents should not be harmed, should not suffer loss of freedom. What right we may speak of was grounded in his innocence, not in his pure humanity. When he kidnaps a star, he leaves the category of innocents and so deserves his harm. The act of kidnapping does not overrule his "right," it voids it. And so there is not the slightest evil in the punishment.

The rights advocate would claim, alternatively, that there is indeed some moral evil in the punishment. After all, there is the denial of a human's right to choose his mode of behavior. Inasmuch as this mode of behavior is harmful to others, we will countenance the evil in punishment rather than accept the greater evil which follows from permissiveness. Two rights square off, so to speak, and one falls at the hand of the other. This is the model for all ethical decision-making. Weigh the various rights and decide which must give way to others. In all this, engineer as little rights loss as possible, recognizing that there is some evil in any such loss. Keep evil to a minimum.

For the matrix theorist, there is not a bit of evil in punishing the kidnapper. There is, indeed, harm, but no evil. Evil lies in victimization, none of which is here. So he has not urged the lesser of two evils. Rather, he, so the account goes, supports a policy without evil. The rights advocate, because he recognizes a host of positive moral entities—rights—sees some evil in punishing even the most loathsome offender. And this is the crux of the matter. Since he sees some evil in most public policy decisions, he is in a good position to move toward support of some policies unacceptable to the matrix theorist. Weighing rights, balancing evils, he can find himself accepting a certain amount of victimization for the sake of avoiding greater victimization. Pushed to the extreme, the rights of Hiroshima schoolchildren can be weighed against the rights of American servicemen in the Pacific and found wanting. Sure, their rights are denied, but that's the sort of thing which happens every time we make a hard, public policy decision. Some rights give way to other rights. And so talk of rights can lead someone to set aside the rule, "Do justice justly," that is, without victimizing. This is the danger in talk of rights.

It should be obvious that many rights advocates would oppose the bombing of Hiroshima. Such talk does not lead inevitably to particular policies. The point is simply this: The concept of human rights can be easily adapted to lesser-of-two-evils thinking, and this sort of thinking is unacceptable for the reasons given earlier in this chapter.

It is best, therefore, to use caution in talking about human rights. Their validity is based upon the rules the matrix contains. The concept of human rights is derivative, not fundamental. Such is also the case for legal rights. Laws are not established to recognize certain legal rights. For there are no legal rights without the laws. The laws generate legal rights. Similarly, moral rules are not based upon human rights. Human rights derive from moral rules. These moral rules, in turn, are based upon human needs. And so it might seem appropriate to go directly from human needs to human rights, skipping or displacing the rules. But, as we have seen, there is danger in putting rights before the rules. There is a restraint in the rules we cannot count upon the rights to supply. The mediating role of rules must be preserved.

Finally, talk of rights puts a strain on the word *deserve*. If an infant has a right to be fed, then we might say he deserves to be fed. But this is not the sense of deserve we find in "Richard

Speck deserves to be punished," or "Our janitor deserves to be paid." These are cases of conscious, significant effort. The infant is incapable of such acts, and so the use of "deserve" in this case is different. By speaking, in the case of the infant, of the prevention of undeserved harm rather than of deserved benefit, we maintain a helpful conceptual sharpness.

4
Statute and Administrative Law

The matrix is simple though I hope not simplistic. It presents broad categories for handling all matters of public policy. It is a large-scale map, only a few of whose details have appeared as yet. The aim of the next two chapters is to fill in some of these details. Throughout the following discussion of specific public affairs issues, I will make use of the broad concepts already explained. In fact, the concepts will be clarified and developed as well as used. These are tough, borderline judgments to make, which will force conceptual analysis.

It won't work to turn to the Bible for direct answers to the bulk of the issues at hand. You cannot quote chapter and verse on handgun control, zoning, compulsory education, affirmative action, and mandatory retirement age. Perhaps, though, this claim underestimates human ingenuity. One could read zoning into the division of Palestine among the twelve tribes and handgun control into the passage on beating swords into plowshares. But this technique isn't very promising, particularly when you consider matters which were technologically unthinkable in biblical times. Psychosurgery and nuclear warfare lie beyond the consciousness of biblical writers, and it is difficult to read direct answers to the problems they raise. This is not, of course, to suggest that the Bible leaves us without answers to the problems. Rather, the answers are implicit in more general formulations. The principles are available for the judgments. The specific issues, then, are settled by appealing to more general principles grounded in Scripture. And so there will be very little

Scripture quoted in the last two chapters. The scriptural base is already laid.

The division between the next two chapters is somewhat arbitrary since the same issues are touched in all branches of government. For example, Congress declares war, the President serves as Commander in Chief, and the courts rule on certain forms of conscientious objection. It is sometimes a matter of historical accident which branch takes the lead in public policy formation; there is nothing in the order of government which ensures that Brown *vs.* Board of Education will precede the Civil Rights Act. A change in policy may originate with OSHA, a federal district court, the Ways and Means Committee of the House of Representatives, or the president. So it is misleading to designate a certain issue as a matter for the courts, or as a matter for the legislature. In light of these few comments, you should not be misled by the classification which follows.

The division, arbitrary though it may be, is intended to show two main ways in which the principle of justice can be applied. First, it can be used to establish broad, standing programs supported by sizable budgets and overseen by a variety of agencies. Second, justice may be applied to particular controversies. Here it is more reactive than formative. The first sort of application will be discussed under the heading, "Statute and Administrative Law," the second under "Case Law."

Regardless of where the policy is shaped or under what circumstances a change is forced, justice should rule. The state is first and last an instrument of justice. Whether we read the *Federal Register*, the *Congressional Record*, the *Northwest Reporter*, or the *Illinois Constitution*, we should find justice at work.

Taxation

There is a similarity between income tax and a holdup; in both cases, the person is told, "Give me your money or I'll harm you."

But the connection is specious, as it must be if taxes are just. Regardless of the good intentions of the holdup man, he uses unjust means. He might, for example, plan to distribute the money to the poor. But in doing you undeserved harm, he does justice unjustly. Is this what occurs when the state takes my money and gives it to the poor in the form of welfare?

There is an essential difference, best understood in terms of insurance. While the thief gives me nothing in return, my tax money funds programs which cover me. If I fall into poverty, I will be helped. The military defends me. The police and courts secure my property rights. In short, I get a significant return on my money. Naturally, I may go through life without needing welfare, but I need not resent this. The man who stays healthy does not begrudge his term insurance premiums, although he never sees them again.

It might be argued that the coverage is all well and good, but that there is a key difference between taxes and insurance premiums. You may elect to go without insurance coverage, but taxes are inescapable. But there is another key difference which offsets this qualification. You enjoy the state's "coverage" long before you make choices at all, and so long as you remain in the state, you enjoy the coverage in the form of defense and legal security. Unlike the thief's, the state's requirement is not harmful; that is, it does not involve loss of freedom. On the contrary, it secures freedoms for the taxpayer. So it's not a matter of doing harm to someone for another's good. No harm is done as long as the money is applied to programs which serve everyone.

There are limits placed upon taxation by the principle of justice. Lest the levy fall into the holdup category, the taxpayer must not suffer harm—loss of freedom. Any tax which is so stiff that it causes deterioration of the individual's basic powers of personhood is harmful. This harm could, for instance, come in the form of malnutrition or exposure. If the taxpayer cannot afford food and shelter, then he is harmed regardless of how secure he is militarily.

The second limit to taxation concerns the use of collected money. Whenever the money is not converted into coverage for the taxpayer, he suffers genuine loss. If some money goes to build a castle for the Secretary of Commerce, then there is net shrinkage in the taxpayer's world. It is, no doubt, in the public interest that the secretary of commerce have a comfortable dwelling. If he is distracted by the inconveniences of poor housing, he will serve us less effectively; and he does need a nice place to entertain other policymakers; social gatherings promote understanding and cooperation. Perhaps the state even needs to provide unusually nice housing to attract key men to the position. But a castle constitutes needless extravagance. The taxpayer's freedoms are not secured by this spending. The rule for public spending is, then, that it must go toward coverage for each taxpayer, directly or indirectly. The same thing goes for charitable projects. If the money is designated, not for all poor people, but only for poor people who happen to be of Irish origin, then the taxpayer is treated unjustly, unless he is Irish. If the Lithuanian-American has no prospects of relief in case of poverty, then his tax to rescue Irish-American unfortunates is unjust. It would be as if a holdup man with a soft spot for the Irish were robbing Lithuanians to fund his favorite charity.

As noted already, every citizen inescapably enjoys certain forms of coverage, such as military defense. No one is in a position to revoke that coverage for the sake of a personal tax savings. But could a citizen exempt himself from welfare coverage? He would, in writing, assume the risk of poverty, judging that he can maintain an acceptable standard of living. In return for this sacrifice, he would be free from a proportionate part of his tax burden. And might he also relinquish police and fire protection, relying upon his own surveillance and equipment? Why not? Why may he not refuse to buy insurance, thereby assuming the risks?

There is a fundamental flaw in this sort of calculation. It employs a sort of "self-made man" concept. Our adventuresome taxpayer figures that the only inescapable coverage he enjoys comes from the military. He is oblivious to the organic structure of society. He does not realize that the very rules which permit him to gain and maintain wealth stand by virtue of the assent of the populace. In short, he enjoys a comfortable life because the people permit it. His riches have no necessary connection with his virtue, desert, or intelligence. Luck, scarcity, and greed are frequently instrumental in gaining wealth. Society may write the rules so that one may profit from luck and scarcity, but this is a matter of convention, not desert or justice. That convention can change if certain organs become parasitic. In cold terms, welfare payments provide coverage for the comfortable no less than does military spending. If there were no welfare for down-and-outers, there would very likely be revolution. Victims, if not supported, lose their gracious spirit toward fortunates, whose fortunes they have secured by their support of certain laws and practices.

One might respond that this reduces the demands of justice to simple prudence and social utility. Welfare is treated, not as a matter of compassion, but as a way of buying off the poor, so they won't murder the well-to-do in their beds. But this objection ignores the basic point of justice made above. The principles of justice are designed for the well-being of society. Antirevolutionary measures may be quite compatible with the well-being of society. If there is bloodshed and turmoil, then society is not healthy, nor are her people happy. None of this crowds out compassion. We simply went beyond ordinary compassion to the hard facts of the matter in order to answer the compassionless adventurer. I may perfectly well pay my taxes compassionately rather than resentfully. My feelings of compassion could be directed toward unfortunates alone, or they might extend to all of society since a revolt of the poor would plunge us all into chaos.

To develop this theme a bit more, welfare serves to do more than pacify the poor. It also helps reduce the meanness of competition among those not receiving welfare. If businessmen know that there is no reliable form of relief to catch them if their business collapses, then a sort of desperation infects the market-place. It makes for war, not competition. A do-or-die atmosphere makes for rough business. Finally, a society which does not care for its poor develops emotional callouses which diminish its capacity for happiness. Perhaps there are other things at stake here, but I hope the point is clearly made. Welfare is vital to all citizens, whether they receive it or not, and so there are no grounds for exempting fortunate taxpayers from supporting it.

Writers on justice have given a good deal of attention to the question of what forms taxes should take. Should they, for instance, be regressive, progressive, or proportional? Is the ordinary sales tax unjust because the poor must pay a greater percentage of their income than the rich to handle it? Is it just to hit the wealthy at a higher rate than the rest of society? The questions go on and on. But on the model presented in this work, no form of taxation is unjust as long as what amounts to a single criterion is met: Nobody is harmed. As discussed above, the harm can come in the form of taxation which cuts into the basics for life or in the form of extraneous government spending. As long as all the money taken goes toward enhancing my freedom, the rate is immaterial. When my taxes forward justice, they serve me, and I am treated justly. No harm, no injustice.

Once we see that the various forms of taxation are morally satisfactory, we can work at generating the largest world by means of them. We might, for example, choose a progressive income tax so that a moderate amount of discretionary spending power will be widely distributed. In this society, many would live fairly well while very few would live extravagantly. The pos-sibility of owning enormous wealth would be effectively elimi-nated. And this possibility might be significant to a good many people. It might just be the case that a society without a generous sprinkling of Rockefellers, Vanderbilts, and Hunts is one which forgets how to dream. A proportional income tax might lengthen rather than broaden society's freedoms. Here the middle class would bear more of the tax burden, but they would have more chance of becoming quite wealthy. So long as nobody is harmed by the taxes, economists and kibitzers can dicker with the rates and modes to their delight. This harm to avoid is simply a net loss of freedom for a person. You might say it becomes a question of whether we want a short fat world or a long lean one.

Regardless of the tax system chosen, it should be established incrementally and treated conservatively. Spasmodic shifts in the tax laws would traumatize investors, whether they be car buyers or mutual funds. This loss of confidence in the future would shackle citizens. Although there might be nothing unjust in my paying half again as many taxes as I now do, if I never know whether, when, and how quickly it's coming, I am harmed. I refrain from taking any loans for fear a new tax rate will ruin me. I rent rather than buy a home, I lease rather than buy a car, and so on. In short, I can only enjoy those freedoms granted me by the tax system if I can reasonably assume the system to be stable. Whatever changes are made in the system should come gradually so that the populace will have time to adjust.

Our present tax system serves many nonfiscal purposes. The host of exemptions and deductions encourage and discourage selected practices. The interest deduction for home buyers obviously encourages this sort of investment; tax-free status for churches offers them a measure of protection, while an excess wage settlement tax could discourage firms from granting inflationary wage increases. These are all instances of taxation for the sake of more than money. As far as this book's model is concerned, these practices are not in principle unjust. The government has the leeway to act in what it perceives to be the public interest, as long as nobody is harmed undeservedly. Now it might seem that an increased tax burden amounts to a harm: money is taken away; planned trips to Europe are cancelled; investment in a new business is frustrated.

The vacation and investment plans are indeed harmed, but the money taken is applied to the project of ensuring the very possibility of vacations and investments. The man may not be able now to make the investment, but had not his money and the money of others gone into public spending, those planned investments could not have succeeded. Investments require laws and stability which require tax support. In the spirit of Hobbes, we might remind that angry taxpayer of the grim alternatives. This is, of course, not to say that taxes may not be unjust or harmful. Rather, the point is this: Taxes are not harmful simply because they disrupt your plans. Unless they are spent wastefully and impertinently, they undergird your very capacity to make plans. This is not a case then of harming the innocent for a greater good, for nobody receives net harm.

Finally, we might think that some of the very rich pay more than they can recover in benefits and so suffer net loss of freedom. On the insurance model, this might mean paying one hundred dollars a year to cover the possible loss of a fifty-dollar piece of silver. We might imagine that the insurance company scales its rates so that the rich compensate for the lower and insufficient premiums of the poor. Some pay five dollars for fifty dollar coverage while others pay one hundred dollars for the same coverage. Surely this would be unjust.

With taxes, however, the coverage is inestimably great. The "premiums" cannot begin to exceed the benefits one does enjoy and may come to enjoy within a just society.

Wages

You will recall that I made use of the *lex talionis* in connection with the category, deserved benefit. We arrived at this standard: Ongoing sustenance for ongoing sustenance. If a person is essential to the life and mission of an institution, then he deserves the essentials himself.

It is hard to see how, on these grounds, any essential job would warrant less pay than any other essential job. If the position is indispensable, then it sustains the life of the institution, and the institution owes it life-supporting pay. A college, for example, cannot dispense with its fund raisers, its faculty, its computer

operators, its plumbers, its residence hall directors, its administrators, and its bookkeepers. Each of these positions contributes
to the body as a significant organ. The body errs if it fails to
sustain, in turn, these organs so that they are not hampered or
distracted by shortages. In short, they deserve a living wage.

The concept, living wage, is not a new one. Philosophers and
economists have batted it around for a good while. Some point to
the vagueness of the expression; what, after all, are the essentials? You might consider a diet of soup sufficient while I might
insist upon frequent and substantial cuts of meat. You might insist
upon at least one trip a month to the movies. Your clothing
interests might involve only protection while I might insist upon
some sensitivity to fashion. The tug-of-war over wants and needs
is an old one.

Still, with all this controversy, there is an intuitive region of
agreement. Virtually everyone would place a living age between
five and twenty thousand dollars today. Even this broad spread
rules out a considerable range of salaries. We are not totally at sea
in making the call. In fine tuning the figure, we should show
sensitivity to cultural survival as well as physical survival. If, for
example, burlap clothing and the lack of a car effectively took a
person out of the employment market and broke up his social
interaction, then they would constitute a genuine harm. This
varies from society to society. A person in this situation in, say,
Tierra del Fuego might not be disadvantaged. He is much more
likely to be in trouble in Los Angeles or Chicago. The living
wage then is keyed to a particular culture. The question to ask is
whether or not the employee will face a deterioration of his
freedom of choice because of the wage; will he lose ground on his
peers? Will he lack a strong base of support from which to move
in shaping his life? Will he be in a position to become sufficiently
familiar with the world to work in it with some success? Does he
have some mobility, some access to education, some capacity to
entertain others, thereby building supportive social relationships?
These are the sorts of questions that ought to figure into the

judgment of what constitutes a living wage, ongoing sustenance for effective personhood.

In speaking of sustenance in exchange for sustenance, we might consider the distinction between essential positions and essential individuals. While the position of philosophy professor might be essential to a college, the particular person filling that position might not be essential. There might be scores of other philosophers who could fill the same position competently. In contrast, a particular plumber might be indispensable because he is the only one familiar with the college's quirky, Byzantine plumbing system. If he were to pass from the scene, the college would be at the mercy of her pipes until someone else could figure them out. Does the plumber then deserve a special wage because of his personal importance?

The answer is *no* because the essential individual and the essential position are both cut from the cloth of circumstance. The plumber is essential because he happens to work for an institution with a poorly constructed and documented plumbing system. In fact, his own failure to chart the system has contributed to his indispensability. If an ambitious apprentice learns the system, the old plumber is instantly dispensable as he might be if the college decides to install a new system. The same can be said for a position. The minute the college subscribes to an independent computer service, the resident computer workers become dispensable. And if the college decides to drop her philosophy course requirement, one of her philosophy professors might become dispensable. This is, again, a matter of circumstance. The essential nature of an individual and of a position is always subject to review. And so the indispensable individual deserves no special salary consideration. The important word here is *deserves*. He may well command a high salary because of the leverage he enjoys. The college may be willing to pay a great sum to keep him, if that's what it takes. They may even want to heap money upon him in gratitude for his help. But his desert is simply that of one among other circumstantial essentials.

Among the most curious arguments to be found are those in support of the claim that one deserves a much higher wage than the other full-time employees. This is not to say that there are no good reasons for wage scales with substantial differences between top and bottom. But to justify this spread in terms of desert takes some doing.

If the justifying criteria, that is, responsibility, pressure, and preparation were consistently applied, there would have to be upheaval in institutional wage policy. A good campus carpenter's preparation is often as extensive as a professor's. The pressure on a junior professor in his first semester or when he's facing a tenure decision equals or surpasses that of any administrator. As for responsibility, while the administrator's is broad, it is quite shallow. Of course, he is accountable for what happens in the eight o'clock philosophy class, but his accountability for that class does not begin to approach the professor's. One is superficially responsible for many things. The other is deeply responsible for a few.

One basis for some differentiation in pay has its physical analogue. Some organs, such as the brain and the liver, require more blood to function properly. So, too, there are workers whose needs are greater. There is a sense in which the professional is never off work. His job calls for continual reflection and attention; he carries his work through weekends and vacations, if only in his head. If his pay does not secure for him the "leisure" he needs to meet his performance standards, then he is treated unjustly. On these grounds, it is just to pay the teacher and the administrator more than the receptionist.

More will be said below in the section on prices. But let me suggest at this point that the standard, extended wage scale is based less on desert than on incentives, concessions, tribute, and pride. It may be minimally workable and excusable, but it is not morally necessary or even important.

Turning to government policy, we see the need for minimum wage legislation. The state makes the best judgment call it can on a living wage and divides it by a reasonable work rate to determine an appropriate wage rate. If, for instance, Congress decides that two hundred dollars a week is a living wage and that a forty-hour week is reasonable, then the minimum wage would be set at five dollars an hour. This example makes use of easy round numbers and isn't meant to proclaim the proper standard.

At this point the economists step in and accuse the philosopher of meddling where he doesn't belong. "Don't you know that minimum wage legislation drives up the cost of business, inflating prices and even killing business? These two effects undermine the very institution of wages, putting many on relief." Three answers come readily to mind. First, if the minimum wage principle is truly a matter of justice, then it is workable since the principle comes from a loving, omniscient father. Second, economics has no more certainty than meteorology and is in no position to be arrogant. Third, our economy has coped with minimum wage legislation for decades. The cost of oil and upper wage levels seem to pose a far more serious threat than the minimum wage. No doubt there are other things to be said for and against the minimum wage, but so far as I can see, my model has nothing else to add—ongoing sustenance for ongoing sustenance.

In many communities, there are those willing to work at full-time, essential jobs for less than a living wage. In a college community, for example, the wives of professors and staff members are available at a lower rate. Their spouses bring home a living wage, and so they are able to work for less. What harm is there in this? It's pretty clear that the working wife is not harmed because she enjoys a comfortable life on the basis of the pooled salaries. But the harm in wages is not always done to the actual employee. The harm in this case is to others in the job market. By taking the lower salary, the employee closes that job to a good many workers who do not enjoy the benefit of a second income. An undersupported job is a curb on the freedom of job hunters. They are excluded for reasons not touching their qualifications.

The employer, seeking savings, is, of course, inclined to take someone up on an offer to work for a less-than-just wage. The comfortable, sacrificial, or desperate employee is also happy to go along with the wage. This collaboration, though pleasing to the parties, short-circuits the system of equal opportunity to a just wage sought by the government. In these cases, the minimum wage requirement must not be relaxed—essentials for essentials.

Similar harm is done by a wage policy which ties pay to actual rather than average needs. If, for instance, single workers are paid less than married workers because they don't have families to support, then singles have an advantage in the job market. Employers will likely seek the cheaper worker, in effect penalizing married people. Again, the employee would not be harmed, for he has the job at a decent wage. The harm would be done to the class of married citizens, outside looking in. This policy, in short, would limit the freedom of married persons. The minimum wage, then, should be keyed to one-worker, moderately-sized families. To do otherwise would discriminate against broad segments of the working force.

It's clear that some businesses could succeed if they were permitted to pay substandard wages. A lot of the success of foreign produced goods lies with the availability of cheap labor. It's difficult to compete when you are obliged to pay decent wages to your employees. It would be marvelous if we could relax the laws, giving business a boost. But it would be equally marvelous if one could go into oil exploration without a huge outlay for equipment. Just think of the oil business without the need to pay for seismographic equipment and exploratory drilling equipment. And just imagine the reduction in overhead for a shirt manufacturer if he could work outdoors year round. The cost of shirts would drop, sales would boom, everyone would be happy. But these are silly cases; certain costs are simply unavoidable. Anyone going into these businesses must pay them. If he can't afford them, then that's too bad. Why can't the cost of workers be viewed in the same manner? If you can't handle the living wage, then you're in no position to go into business. It would be marvelous to cut costs, but certain costs are set.

Finally, a word about wages for youth. As is the case for working wives, the young person seldom bears the responsibility of supporting a family. He doesn't need the full living wage, but if he could be paid less, he would be a more attractive employee and would block older people from the market. There is, though, a check on this obstruction. The young person's working hours may be limited by both the state and school requirements. This would force him into a part-time status, freeing full-time employment for adults. Despite this check, however, there would still be a block to the freedom of fellow citizens, because adults, too, have an interest in the part-time market. If it were permissible to pay lower wages to a young part-time employee, then I, as an adult, would likely be blocked from working at a place like McDonalds. So regardless of their special status, a living wage, or the minimum wage should be paid to young people, too, as long as their part-time work plays an essential role in the company.

Welfare

Welfare is for genuine victims. It is not given because the recipients deserve it, for they have done nothing significant for others. Rather, they have been harmed undeservedly and that state of harm is unacceptable. The state acts to restore the freedom lost to its citizens by misfortune. As discussed under taxation, the money used for welfare is taken from what amounts to poverty insurance premiums paid by others. The money is no more "down the drain" for those not receiving welfare than it would be for those who live despite their having term life insurance. In both situations, the coverage stands.

The purpose of welfare is to restore and preserve the freedom of a person who is unable to do so himself. This purpose reads like the purpose of a living wage. It, too, is designed to supply the base for personhood, the essentials. Both welfare and a living wage are designed for sustenance then. And so it would follow that welfare should be paid at the minimum wage rate. This is a hard saying because it presents the image of two men, one working and the other not working, receiving the same income. Where is the justice in this? Why should the worker bother if he can get the same income doing nothing?

This specter is avoidable, though, through proper design and administration of the program. It must be emphasized that only genuine victims would receive welfare. And of those victims, those who are able to work can be assigned to government projects. If the person either is unable to find regular employment or refuses government work or simply refuses to seek regular employment, then he is out of luck. He must take what is available. If there is absolutely nothing available, then he qualifies as a *bona fide* victim and help should be given him. This approach eliminates the prospect of parasitic deadbeats.

A key part of the program is what is sometimes called *workfare*. There are many public-service tasks available at any given time. Vacant lots need cleaning, roads need patching, the elderly need home maintenance help, and high crime neighborhoods can use more surveillance. When the other job market is closed off, the unemployed could be put to work on these projects. There is, of course, a checkered history of such projects, from the Civilian Conservation Corps to CETA. Sometimes they are useful, but at other times they are a mockery. Poorly supervised, they turn into havens for listless people. Fearing loss of government funding, local administrators retain their useless workers, thereby poisoning the morale of their crews and wasting the taxpayers' money. But there is no reason why the programs need be poorly administered. The standards of industry could be applied to this sort of work. If a man is shirking, he can be fired, and if fired from public-work projects, he is ineligible for welfare; he cannot be called a victim. His harm is deserved. He is more the fool than the victim. If he finds the work to be unfulfilling and so rejects it, he may be treated as a finicky pet. If the food is decent, and he refuses it, then he does without until he decides that perhaps it is not so bad after all. Finally the workfare force is not a fixed group, but one which flexes to match the current job market. When there are jobs available and men qualified, then they may not remain under workfare.

There are persons, of course, who cannot enter the workfare force. Children and the physically disabled, for example, are unable to contribute significantly in return for their aid. Nevertheless, they should be decently supported. To do otherwise would be to accept their victimization.

The economist might reply that these policies would impose a drag on the economy. Such a generous level of welfare would present a heavy burden to the taxpayers. By trimming welfare, enough money is left for widespread investment and discretionary spending. The answer to this is plain and simple; an economy which prospers at the expense of the victimization of a segment of society is unjust. If justice, as has been argued, is ultimately a matter of human well-being, then those adopting this policy undermine society in the long run. Injustice will catch up with you.

This scheme would serve both to increase welfare payments and tighten up eligibility. As it now stands, welfare is both substandard and fairly easily available. In my judgment it should be both more rewarding and harder to get. The whole scheme turns upon the concept of victimhood. Welfare is more a defensive policy than one which funds the dearest plans of its recipients. It is an anti-victimization program only. And so it is of no concern to us that a welfare recipient is unable to buy an expensive car. We are not at all responsible to assume the cost of such as that. We underwrite only the essentials. He will have to pass up Chicago's near north lakefront and settle for less exciting quarters. The public is not obliged to pay whatever bills he may want to incur. There are limits established by the minimum wage.

The minimum wage is designed to support a modest family,

say of two children. Those wishing more must turn to part-time work, moonlighting, or working spouses. It's not the employer's responsibility to fund the Trapp family. He is in charge of the essentials, and a large family is not an essential. Let's turn this standard now toward welfare recipients. With the same concern for essentials, we support a modest family on welfare. But when the welfare family or mother has additional children, society is sent additional bills. Each new child increases our financial burden by thousands of dollars. Procreation, particularly under these circumstances, is an act with public consequences.

Irresponsible procreation by welfare recipients serves to raise the insurance premiums for all. Of course, the coverage may well be extended to all; if they find themselves on welfare, they, too, may overprocreate. But in this case, that's more coverage than they want and need. It is as though the insurance company penalizes all policy holders by awarding generous settlements to reckless drivers. Their graciousness drives premiums up, reducing the freedom of the policy holders. And this increased cost does not come in the interest of justice. A couple is not victimized if they are limited to two children any more than they are victimized if they are limited to cars in the Pinto price range. So those on welfare who go on to have large families are harming society. They bill us for their excesses.

How can this practice be met? Surely not by refusing to support the children. They did not ask to be born and to short them would victimize them. They would be paying for someone else's sins. If we're already paying for the essentials and a new child comes along, then it is reasonable to increase payments. This is what we, at present, do, and it may encourage procreation—more children, more money; but the answer is not to deny the help. What about penalizing the parents? Perhaps by jailing or fining them, others will be discouraged from such excesses. But again, this would victimize the child. The family can only afford the essentials anyway. Any fine would cut into the support for the child, and imprisonment would take the parents out of the home, depriving the child of that important relationship. The parents deserve some sanction, but it should not be administered in such a way as to victimize others, in this case the children.

One answer would be to treat extended child support as a loan rather than a direct welfare grant. The debt is incurred by the father or, if he is not to be found, the mother. This debt may be paid either in terms of public-works service or cash. If the family or mother comes off the welfare rolls, then the money taken above the living wage plus extra child costs may be called in by the state. If this is not possible, then as time becomes available without harm to the children, workfare overtime can be assessed. Society extends a loan, for the sake of the children, to irresponsible parents. The parents have billed society for a luxury and someday they must pay.

This scheme would discourage absent fathers since, in their absence, the mothers assume the debts. This would encourage them to name the fathers. It would also discourage prolific procreation by putting a price tag on the practice. It would proclaim the truth that man has no inviolable right to procreation according to his own wishes. Procreation is a public as well as a private concern; it can foist a responsibility upon others, thereby limiting their freedoms undeservedly. Under some circumstances procreation could be viewed as a public offense. It is just for society to determine the essentials for a family and to refuse to bankroll more than this.

No doubt it is tricky business to determine the essentials, the living wage, which lie at the heart of minimum wage and welfare programs. There is great disagreement over what the basics are. Some parents put their children in day-care centers so that they can have two incomes, enabling them to buy a pleasure boat. Other parents would not think of treating the children in that fashion in order to gain what they judge a luxury. Isn't it presumptuous of the state to decide who is living above standard and to legislate accordingly? It may be presumptuous, but it is no more so than thousands of other judgments made daily by officials of the state. The decisions surrounding the legal expression *negligence* alone are voluminous and equally risky. How may we ever make foreign policy in a changing, surprising world? Decisive judgments in the absence of consensus are the norm in government. Living wage decisions are just another part of the family of tough and necessary decisions the state makes.

Before we move to the next section, I need to show that what seems to be a contradiction in my account is not one at all. In chapter 2, I said that loss of property means loss of freedom. In this section, I said that welfare should restore the freedom that one loses undeservedly. It would seem to follow that welfare must cover all our losses. Yet, I claim that it should meet only the essentials.

Suppose, for example, that lightning hits your million-dollar mansion. It burns to the ground, and you suffer its loss undeservedly. You are a victim of natural forces. As minister to victims, should the state restore your property, thereby correcting injustice? No, this form of welfare would be fantastic and unnecessary. It is entirely appropriate for the state to hold those who would make such investments responsible for securing insurance. It should be understood that this coverage is simply part of the cost of ownership and that those who neglect to secure it are so negligent as to fall outside the category of victims.

Beyond the essentials, we are, so to speak, on our own. Of course, we enjoy police protection and a variety of regulations which make property a workable part of culture. But when it comes to compensation for particular loss of discretionary property, we should provide for ourselves.

Prices

A cluster of concepts lying at the heart of any economic system can be grouped under a variety of headings. Although I have used prices and fees to denote the category, I could have initiated the same discussion under the headings of property, copyright, or monopoly. I write on these issues with a good deal of sheepishness because of my unfamiliarity with the ins and outs of current economic theory. Nevertheless I am convinced that the justice model constructed in this book can address in broad terms the question of what form a just economic system would take. The assumption that the principles of behavior prescribed by a loving God are for our well-being leads me to believe that a just economic system is also a workable and beneficial one. Ethics does not stand over against good business in the final analysis; it directs business to its happiest and most durable form. Just business is, in the long run, good business.

To begin with, we need to distinguish entitlement from desert. I may, for example, agree to give you a thousand dollars in return for the perverse privilege of hitting you in the face with pies. You, in desperate financial difficulties, agree to the humiliation. But it would be odd to say that you deserve this treatment, unless you squandered the plentiful money you had. It would be strange to say I'm giving you what you deserve. This simply does not fit the sense of desert used in talk of deserved harm and benefit. The most that can be said of my act of hitting you with pies is that I am entitled to it. But this entitlement is strictly relative to our agreement and not grounded in the nature of morality. Since the chance to hit someone with a pie cannot be counted among the essentials due me for essential contribution to others, it cannot be said that I deserve the chance to do it.

Similarly, I may agree to give you a million-acre ranch in Texas if you will scratch my back for ten seconds. Your act of back scratching would then entitle you to the ranch. But it just wouldn't make sense to say you deserve the ranch. There is a substantial gap between mere entitlement and the desert of "Al Capone deserves to be punished" and "Hardworking welders deserve to eat."

The line between desert and entitlement follows the line between essentials and niceties. Property straddles this line; some property, a coat for instance, is deserved, while other property, such as a private jet, is not. That property available for commercial transactions is undeserved, for its very availability shows it to be nonessential. If a coat is essential to me, then I am not in a position to sell it for a profit. I might, of course, sell it and buy a cheaper coat with the money and pocket the change, but this sort of transaction falls short of business as we practice it.

The principle of desert does not oblige the state to guarantee the bulk of property we enjoy. We do not really deserve all our holdings. But, as we saw in earlier discussions, the matrix provides a rationale for undeserved ownership, for pure entitlement. The category of undeserved harm comes to the fore here. If the state does not preserve a structure of entitlement, then our freedom is denied. Uncertain of our ability to hold onto those items we come to possess, we despair of making plans beyond the essential matters, such as meals. A system of entitlement provides a way to help us work for our dreams. Whatever the process for accumulating undeserved benefit, there should be one, lest we be harmed by curbs to our freedom.

It would be good here to develop the distinction between limitations and damages. Limitations are either moral or what we might call natural. The moral limitations imposed upon us are the prohibitions found in Scripture—Don't murder; don't steal. The natural limitations simply compose the human condition. Prohibitions and finitude limit us. Although the distinction between moral and natural limitations is useful, it should be clear by now that the moral limitations are themselves natural in that they follow natural laws of human well-being; you cannot violate them without undermining that well-being. They are still distinguishable from those other limitations called natural.

Here are some of the natural limitations we encounter: I am not free to fly with my arms, to memorize the Chicago phone book, to own a diamond the size of a basketball, to be a descendant of Theodore Roosevelt, to live to the age of two hundred, to be the best typist in the U.S. by tomorrow afternoon, or to give all my friends their own planets. These limitations are simply facts of life, not damages. Physical finitude, scarcity, and just plain history rule out certain chances.

Neither form of limitation is a harm. Neither one is an assault on freedom. Both simply serve to define freedom for humans. To be a free human person is to be free under these conditions. They form the arena in which we are to apply the principles of justice. They do not figure into judgments of deserved and undeserved harm, since they are not harms. It would be very odd to sentence a mugger to five years without the freedom to pull himself up by his bootstraps or to compensate a person for his lack of earthly immortality or for his lack of freedom to kill whom he wishes. These simply don't count as harms.

Damages, on the other hand, are harms. I may be damaged by malnutrition, enslavement, renal failure, looting, a crippling attack, and a conspiracy to deny me a restaurant meal because of my color. Each of these represent the imposition of new limitations upon my already limited self. They are forms of loss. Diseases, bigots, thieves, and assailants damage me, reduce my freedom, harm me. They "box me in" in new ways. Of course, not all damages are unjust. The damage a court system does to an offender may be acceptable. It is damage to innocents and excessive damage to offenders which are unacceptable.

Now to bring things together. A just economic system ensures both that workers receive the essentials they deserve and that persons are not damaged by its policies. In this context, the damage would be a loss of freedom to pursue entitlement. The state has no obligation to provide the full range of niceties to everyone; there is a difference between granting you the freedom to acquire a jet and granting you the jet itself.

Imagine a street system with a number of arbitrarily closed streets. An economic system which permits such inaccessibility is a damaging one. There may, of course, be limitations to the public freedom to enter the street. It may be at the top of an extraordinarily steep hill, far out in the country, in the middle of a severe snow belt, or only large enough to accommodate twenty cars; but these obstacles are of a different order from that created by the "street closed" sign. When the sign is erected, I suffer loss of freedom, am damaged. Similar but less extensive damage would be done by signs marked, "Street closed for Blacks" and "Street closed except for Rockefellers." A just economic system then does not say of any benefit and to any person, except offenders, "You can't get there from here." To rule in this fashion would inflict undeserved harm.

We should move now to a more particular determination of the form of such an economic system, one which removes damaging curbs to the freedom of its citizens. Whatever form it takes, it should show sensitivity to limitations of the sort discussed above.

There is, as we shall see, an important distinction to be drawn concerning the ways in which men may attempt to turn a profit. The terms *finite* and *infinite* could serve to designate the two classes. Among the finite things with which a person can do business are iron ore, land, and water. The Bessemer process, the formula for Coca Cola, and Management by Objectives are items with potential for infinite use. By possessing or by having access to these two kinds of things, a person is in a position to do business, to attempt to profit. They provide the road to accumulation of great wealth. It is the task of the state to keep this road open, while honoring the limitations imposed by nature and by morality.

Let's first look to the finite things. No one deserves to own a stock of exhaustible resources. Desert, you will remember, stops at the essentials. Imagine some explorer discovering what is today called the Mesabi Range. How can the mere discovery make him a deserving owner? He may have simply stumbled upon the store of iron ore while doing some landscape painting or hunting. He might have been able to recognize the iron ore because some negligent adviser pushed him into an extraneous geology course in college and because a severe storm has just washed open the side of a mountain. Surely such a chain of happy accidents cannot support a claim of desert.

But what about the man who, making an educated guess, sacrifices ten years of his life to mount an expedition in search of such an iron range. He takes the risks, assumes the costs, gives the time and effort, sacrifices a social life, and so on. Wouldn't he truly deserve to own the range? But what exactly has he done to merit millions or billions of dollars in profit? Taken risks? So has the structural steel worker. Does he deserve millions? Well, he's given time and effort, but so has any working man. Assumed costs? Perhaps the expedition does cost millions, but does he then deserve additional millions? Does this mean that a man who spends great sums obligates the state to underwrite a multiplication of investment? That would be a sweet arrangement but one hardly made in the name of desert. The fact of the matter is, our expedition would have never been launched had not a structure of entitlement already been in place. The expedition would not go out on grounds of desert, hoping to assume the blessed and honorable state of merit. Rather, playing the odds and the entitlement game, they hope to "strike it rich."

But say that the explorer goes on to work the range, "mixing his labor" with it. Does he not by this come to deserve it? Unless people have commissioned him to work the range, it's hard to see how anybody owes him anything, whether it be direct payment or noninterference. Indeed his decision to mix his labor with the mountains could just as well be seen as high-handed. If he mines the range for a time, profiting from it, it is even harder to see in what sense he deserves to possess it. One could argue with equal strength that his use should place him last in line of access. After all, he's had his turn to enjoy its benefits.

Even though it would do violence to the concept, desert, to say our man deserves the range, it would be even stranger to say anyone else does. The head of the expedition may not deserve it, but he has far more warrant to it than a haberdasher in San Antonio who has never heard of it. If the man who found it doesn't deserve it, then nobody does. And that is precisely the state of affairs—nobody deserves it. So what is to be done with it? In the absence of desert, what about entitlement?

Upon discovery, the range joins the list of things of which the citizens are conscious. Their world is enlarged. None of them deserves the ore, but none of them deserves to be denied access to it. Since we don't need to regard it as a wage for someone, we can focus upon preserving everyone's access to the iron, within the limitations. Very simply this is a matter of keeping it available and as affordable as possible. No person should be allowed to sit on the reserves for his own pleasure of possession. Nor should anyone be granted sufficient control to set prices as he pleases. This would enable him to enjoy the income from the iron at the expense of our access to it.

A probable partial answer comes in the form of price controls on the sale of such natural resources. The controls should be set so as to take into account the limitations imposed upon the miner's ability to profit—his costs in wages, equipment, insurance, and so on. The controls should also be sensitive to the amount of profit necessary to make the venture attractive to a businessman, but there cannot be an open-ended approach to profits on exhaustible resources. High profits come from pricing which damages public access to the coal. The loss of freedom, the contraction of the world, caused by a greedy price hike is an undeserved harm to the public. People unable to pay the prices are not free to go get their own iron ore if the supplier's price is too high. If they could do so, then the mining company could be free to price as it pleases. But since the supplies are limited, the consumer would be genuinely "boxed in." The ordinary limitations to his freedom imposed by problems in finding and mining the iron ore would be augmented by the artificial limitations of an excessive profit margin on a diminishing resource.

The state policy on expendable resources need not stop here. There may be a set of priorities in the national interest which, if ignored, could prove harmful to the citizens. If, for example, the government needed a large supply of iron to make a new series of tanks, then the iron could be channeled into defense even though higher bids for the iron came from urban contractors. The way is open for the full range of government control if the national interest demands it. Wartime policies exemplify the most rigorous supervision of natural resources. The principle of taxation fits the situation well—the state may take what it needs to preserve and do justice. As long as this is the use, then those taxed do not suffer net loss or harm.

The same general principles can be applied to the issue of land use. No one deserves a piece of land, but neither do they deserve to be denied it, unless they are offenders. The state is free both to remove artificial limitations to land use and to prescribe what that use will be, in the national interest. While taking care not to harm its citizens by its policies, it should disregard any claims to absolute property rights. Real property is a matter of entitlement, not desert, and the state is the commissioner of entitlement. The system of entitlement might permit very little personal discretion in ownership, but once arrangements have been made under that system, any duplicity on the part of the government is harmful, and so unjust. In other words, the rules set down by the state could be quite restrictive for the citizens, but once in place, they impose restrictions upon the state. Otherwise the citizen loses his freedom to make plans with any hope of success. Whatever design the state deems in the best interest of society, whether it takes the form of the Oklahoma land rush, the Northwest Territory policy, or the visitor policy at Yellowstone, once it is set, it should not be capriciously reversed.

The other class of things useful to the businessman, the infinite things, may be handled somewhat differently. The Bessemer process, for example, can be understood by everyone in the country without loss. That knowledge can be passed down through the generations without depletion. But there are still sticky questions of use and ownership. For the Bessemer process was not described in a God-given booklet in the Garden of Eden. Neither is it inscribed on mountains containing iron ore. It took the work of a person, in this case the nineteenth century Englishman Sir Henry Bessemer to discover the process.

Does the discoverer deserve to own and control the process? How does this differ, if at all, from the Mesabi Range case? The same points about accidents and effort can be made. Some momentous discoveries are also serendipitous. Schoolchildren are told about the accident of the first X-ray photo, how the chance arrangement of materials in the scientist's desk drawers produced the proper alignment for an impression. But even when the discovery takes a good deal of effort and expense, where is desert amounting to control of the information?

It might be argued that the Bessemer process, unlike the Mesabi Range, is the handiwork of a person and was not in the world until the discoverer conceived it. But this sells the world short. Whether Bessemer thought of it or not, oxygen and heat caused combustion. Bessemer simply applied an already existing law or regularity in nature to a new situation. Human inventors must work with given natural materials and laws. They discover the nature of nature as our adventurer discovered the existence of the range. The same sort of thing can be said for those in the social sciences. Whatever techniques there are for dealing with humans individually or in mass depend upon the already existent nature of man.

For the purpose of analogy, we might turn to the public library. Think of the nonfiction holdings. Those books exist because of the efforts of a host of writers who took care to describe a portion of the world. Some came as the result of great sacrifice; *Kon-Tiki,* for instance, involved the writer in a perilous trip across the Pacific. He made the trip for the purpose of proving the theory expressed in the book. Other writers made no special effort to gather or dig out their information; John, author of the *Book of Revelation,* merely had to record what God revealed in a vision. Virtually anyone close to a President of the United States has the makings of a book in the form of reminiscences. These works are available to the public with little or no charge. The writers do not retain control over the information in the books, but they enjoy the royalties. These royalties can serve to cover expenses, reward effort, and attract writers. They do not, however, amount to enough to bar dissemination of the discoveries.

This analogy threatens to break down, not because of dissimilarities, but because of great similarity. Books are often the means by which new information is made profitable. But enough distance remains to continue the analogy. Let's return to Sir Henry Bessemer and construe him as the author of a new book on the manufacture of steel. As an incentive to other inventors and as a sort of finder's fee, we grant him royalties from his book. These royalties are not so steep as to discourage others from making use of the book. If he controls the knowledge without deserving it for himself, then he acts in a manner harmful to society. He artificially limits the freedom of others to work with it. He should not be free to decide who checks out the book, nor should he be able to impose steep costs on those wanting the book. He simply does not deserve that control. Neither do we. However, none of us deserves to be denied access to the book.

This does not prevent people from making money on the readily accessible information. Every library has a book on building houses, but I still call on a builder for help. He does nothing not mentioned in the book, but I don't wish to expend the time and effort needed to master the information. Neither do I have the time or inclination to apply the Bessemer process, so without resentment I let others use that book.

Unlike the Mesabi Range, the Bessemer process is not exhaustible. And so there is no material reason to impose checks on its use. The state does have an interest in imposing checks on checks on its use though. If, so to speak, someone tries to keep the book to himself or even destroy the book out of spite, he should be stopped. This is essentially antimonopolistic action. So long as there is free access to the knowledge, there will be competition or the threat of competition to keep the prices reasonable. If someone tries to make too much from the knowledge, someone else is free to check out the book himself and undercut the prices. If this option is always genuinely open, then the damaging curbs to public freedom of use are broken down. The price reflects the limitations imposed by costs rather than imposing artificial limitations itself. There should be no need for price controls beyond those accomplished by antimonopoly and antiprice-fixing legislation.

Finally, a word about a case constructed in Robert Nozick's *Anarchy, State and Utopia.* He argues that there is nothing unjust in a great many people each paying a small amount of money to see Wilt Chamberlain shoot baskets, even though Chamberlain receives an enormous amount for relatively little effort. With this, I would agree. Although there is some difficulty in fitting the Chamberlain case into my scheme of finite and infinite things, the answer is clear. On the one hand, Wilt Chamberlain is an exhaustible resource; his power to shoot baskets is not infinite. On the other hand, he is the author of the phenomenon; it's not as though he simply discovered himself lying there like the Mesabi Range. Does this mean that we should enjoy control over the spectacle of Chamberlain's court work, just as we control the iron reserves? Are we free to schedule his appearances in major cities so the entire country may enjoy him with little inconvenience? Or should he be treated as a sort of natural law? Neither of these work. But there is an answer in the form of a limitation, a moral limitation. In opening freedoms up to the populace, you must honor physical and moral limitations. The moral violation here would come as undeserved harm to Chamberlain. By forcing his appearances, we would damage his freedom. As desirable as the nationwide tour or telecast might be, it must not be done at the expense of another's freedom. We do not deserve to see him shoot baskets, nor does he deserve to be packaged. As for competition, the way is open. Abdul-Jabbar waits in the wings. If there is no Abdul-Jabbar at hand, there is simply a natural limitation placed on competition; there is only one Wilt. So in cases of individual beauty, talent, or intelligence, the gifted one is free to horde his capacities or exercise them for great profit.

In conclusion, property is a matter of entitlement, not desert. The resources of the earth as well as its laws belong to nobody by virtue of merit; so, in a sense, they belong to everybody—to society—and should be used in the interest of the freedom and well-being of everyone. Artificial bars to access are damaging and so unjust. Only the limitations imposed by nature and morality should prevent this access. While there should be no great profit made on exhaustible resources, the way is clear for enormous profits from infinite resources. Antimonopoly and anticollusion laws stand as a barrier to some but not all wealth. As for the Coca-Cola formula, it, like the Bessemer process, can be an entitlement, but not one which is strictly deserved. It is within moral guidelines for the state to treat it as public property; however, there is certainly no obligation to do this. When Coca-Cola's possession of the formula becomes damaging to the public's freedom to enjoy the drink or to engage in the cola business, then society may rightfully demand that the barrier be removed.

Health Care

A crippling sickness is a harm in that it diminishes the person's freedom to act. If that person is an innocent, then the harm of sickness is undeserved and so, unjust. There might be cases, though, where the sickness satisfied our sense of justice; a terrorist concocting a bacteriological bomb could contract the disease himself. But for the ordinary person, disease constitutes an injustice.

Now it might seem odd to suggest that there is injustice without unjust acts. Disease need not be the result of an act; how can it effect an injustice? Perhaps the reason for the oddness of the thought of germs effecting injustice lies in the context of discussions of justice. Ordinarily we discuss justice with an eye to ordering our behavior or regulating the behavior of others. Justice is predicated of certain acts, institutions, and persons. We aim to act justly and counsel others to do the same. I am suggesting, though, that "just" and "unjust" are applicable not only to acts and persons but also to situations. A situation in which harm or benefit is given to a person is one in which there is an instance of justice or injustice.

It is often said that justice has been done when a crooked businessman is financially ruined, a cruel plot backfires, or a terrorist's bomb explodes while he's planting it. Yet, none of these incidents need be an instance of someone's acting justly. Justice can occur without someone's doing something in the interest of justice. Similarly, injustice can occur without someone's doing something in the interest of injustice.

The governmental health care plan I suggest is limited, though, for it is grounded in opposition to undeserved harm. Inasmuch as sickness can be deserved, the government has no responsibility to care for all those who are sick. There are certain clear steps you can take to make yourself sick. If you intentionally and freely drink lye, you will be harmed, but this harm is not undeserved. There is a morally relevant difference between my getting sick by choice and my getting sick by accident. Since some sickness is not undeserved, some sickness is not unjust and does not call for state action.

There is very high correlation between drinking lye and becoming ill; there is significant, though somewhat less, correlation between other practices and illness—cigarette smoking and lung cancer, heavy drinking and cirrhosis of the liver, overeating and heart disease, promiscuity and venereal disease, auto racing and trauma. The risk is high here; the probability of harm is substantial. If one engages in these practices and then becomes sick, then there is an element of desert present. Accordingly, the harm is not unjust if you knew the risk was high. When the risk is high and the person knows the risk, then it is inappropriate to designate the harm received as undeserved.

What does this mean in terms of governmental policy? The government will help those who become sick innocently and will not help those who, having the pertinent information at hand, make themselves sick. The authorities could catalog and publicize unsafe practices. If sickness occurs in the absence of these practices, then the government steps in to help. If the citizen wishes to take the risks, then he is responsible for ensuring himself. In short, you ought not be required to pay for my cure if I've chosen to make myself ill.

The program might well go like this. The surgeon general's office determines that smoking, among other practices, is risky, and the statement is made that heavy smokers contracting lung cancer will not receive benefits. The list need not be definitive, for there are countless ways to harm yourself. Still, the list could indicate the borderline cases and common, risky practices. It could clearly show the principle to be applied to unlisted cases. Of course, the stakes would be high, and the temptation to deceive would be there, so the person seeking the health care benefits would need to justify his claim that his illness is undeserved; perhaps an affidavit from his doctor coupled with submission to simple tests would suffice. For example, there might be some trace of heavy tobacco use in the skin or blood, or on the teeth. The administration of the program, of course, could be complicated and there would be errors, but this need not disqualify such a program. After all, the administration of criminal justice has its problems, but we don't argue that it's not worth the effort. In matters of justice, you just do the best you can. The goal is simply that those who become ill despite acting responsibly should be cared for.

With regards to overeating, the government would probably choose to construct age/height/build/weight tables to use in rulings on heart problems. If a person chooses to become or remain overweight, then he exempts himself from certain health care coverage. Of course, suitable exemptions could be arranged for those with genetic or glandular problems.

When the government issues a warning, its effect on the health care program should not be retroactive. For example, if cyclamates are found to be dangerous, a person is not held responsible for his consumption of cyclamates before the discovery was made. Knowledge is a necessary element in desert. Only if he consumes cyclamates after the announcement is he held accountable.

Now this whole plan might smack of blackmail by health enthusiasts or teetotalers or perhaps another instance of Big Brotherism, with the government interfering with our eating and drinking habits. Perhaps it is seen as a gun to the head or a carrot on a stick. It would be foolish to deny that this approach would give comfort or even a grim satisfaction to some. Of course, it could well drive some people to abstinence of various sorts. But these things are beside the point. The program is not the special-interest legislation of pietists and physical culturalists. The focus is not on sin but on the suffering of innocents. The program is one of giving, not taking away. It is instituted in the interest of correcting injustice.

A word needs to be said about activities such as automobile driving and coal mining. Both involve risks, and yet it would be unfair to deny aid to all accident victims. Some allowance needs to be made for the requirements of day-to-day living, of commerce, of employment. We need to drive; coal miners need to work. The laws need to be reasonable. Still, some distinctions could be honored concerning these activities. If driving or behavior in the mines is reckless, then the element of desert in harm is greater and benefits should be denied. If, however, in a somewhat risky but important activity, one is careful, then his harm is undeserved enough to be unjust.

If the minimum wage and welfare rates were set at a level sufficient to handle a full range of medical insurance premiums, then the responsibility for paying them would rest in the private sector. Alternatively, we could establish a comprehensive national plan. Both approaches would address the injustice of disease without doing injustice to the people. As long as the tax money went for coverage, then there would be no genuine loss to the taxpayers. If the former approach were used, then care would need to be taken to cover those victimized by others' irresponsibility; a child should not lack coverage simply because a parent failed to ensure him, choosing instead to buy a snowmobile. These details could be worked out.

Obviously, a loss of power or freedom to act is inevitable as aging occurs. Movement is impaired, memory fails, bones become brittle, and tissues break down. If these things were to happen as the result of another's actions, we would clearly charge him with harmful acts. If my attack upon you were to cause some loss of memory and mobility, then I might face criminal charges as well as a suit for damages. Without a culprit, this sort of loss occurs daily among aging people.

In most cases, then, aging is unjust. If we could arrest or reverse it by means of medication, then we would be obliged to do so. But we just do not have this capacity. So we should count aging as an aspect of the human condition. Old age and death are not suitable targets for those who would see justice done. Instead they frame and delimit the arena in which we are to perform justly. The injustice of aging is so pervasive and unavoidable that we would do well to treat it as a natural limitation and not a harm.

The aim of a just health care plan is the maintenance and restoration of basic role-playing capacity. The principle extends to the handicapped at birth. When their condition is such that they cannot secure the essentials of life, when the effects of, say thalidomide, are so grave as to render them helpless, we must not let them die.

The obvious objection to all this talk of health care is the cost. It's one thing to advocate widespread health care and quite another thing to pay for it. The first response is to repeat an important theme of this book—if it serves justice, then it is a workable and beneficial policy. We help the afflicted because we are instructed to do so, and we trust God to sort out the consequences. The second response is an equally familiar qualification—do justice justly. Don't victimize in caring for victims.

Let's look at a contrived example. Imagine that we discover a very expensive cure for multiple sclerosis. An individual dose is refined from fifty tons of a special ore found only on the moon. For each small injection of the antidote, we must send a space shuttle to the moon and back several times. Once all expenses are totaled, we find each treatment to run $100 million. Does justice demand that we pay this price to arrest and correct the disease's crippling influence? After all, we, too, would be covered in case of MS. So doesn't this fit the just tax system? Probably not.

When the tax cuts into our own essentials, then we are harmed. When the cost of justice becomes so high that we are harmed in underwriting it, then we should not continue. If, for example, in fighting MS we are unable to afford food for our families, then we have gone too far. But does this mean that we should fund health care up to the point that all we have are the essentials? Should all income over the living wage be taken by the state for the sake of expensive cures? No, for this would harm us all. It would effectively erase our cultural prospects. Stripped to the basics, none of us could enjoy travel abroad, large families, or a fine local symphony. For these sorts of things rely upon discretionary income or patronage. It is not vital that all of us enjoy these things. It is vital that they be possibilities. The structure of entitlement should be so constructed and maintained as to provide for a wealth of opportunities. We must keep open the way for more than survival. To fail in this regard would be a blow to freedom, a harm. So health care must not come at the expense of dreams and culture; in the final analysis, they, too, are essentials. A people cannot afford to lose their arts and sciences.

Despite these qualifications, a national program of care for the afflicted can seem overpowering. Yet there is room for talk of another sort of care. We've considered what amounts to lifesaving care for citizens who are responsible toward their own bodies. And we've made room for treatment which prevents or restores lost power. But this leaves room for another sort of concern.

If I strike you, damaging your brain, and so cause a loss of memory and mental quickness, I harm you. Your role-playing capacity is diminished. You are limited to a smaller world. For example, this eliminates your chances to be an air-traffic controller at D-FW. I should be punished for my deed, and you should be given corrective care, if any can be found. But what about the person who comes into this world with a weak memory and a slow mind? He, too, is restricted to a smaller world. Is it the state's responsibility to do what it can to enhance his mental power? Similarly, must it provide sophisticated prosthetic devices for the congenitally deformed? Must we equip the congenitally blind with expensive, portable image enhancers? These latter people have suffered no loss of power. They simply never had it.

Who then has the essentials? If the congenitally slow-minded person has the essentials, then why are we bothered when the attacker takes you to his level? If the congenitally slow person is short of essentials, then how may we let him languish at that level if treatment is possible? Which is the appropriate standard? The answer involves world size.

The standard or essential allotment of freedom is keyed to that which the world has to offer. Anything less than freedom of access to everything in the "world" of my state is a harm. If I do not have the freedom to become an air-traffic controller, then I suffer harm. Whether this is the case because of kidnapping, birth defect, or racial prejudice, I am unjustly limited. In these cases, I am a victim because my freedom is in check.

What then is the proper state response? Place me at the console at D-FW immediately? Of course not. This is not what justice requires. It is not the actuality of but the freedom to pursue the job which is at issue. But say we discover a chemical which will break down the neural barriers to mental quickness. Imagine that we find a drug which will increase IQ to the air controller level. Is it the state's responsibility to supply this drug to all who could benefit by it? Is it our task to make everyone's world as large as possible? It would seem that the justice described above demands it.

But it might be objected that this policy would involve unjust means. The argument would go as follows: Recall the treatments of taxation and welfare. A tax is just if the taxpayer enjoys a return—coverage. He must not suffer net world shrinkage. He must be eligible for the care he sustains in the case of welfare. But in this case, he would not enjoy coverage. By the time he is taxable, his congenital state is already established. While he may in the future suffer loss of power from sickness or injury, he does not face the prospect of congenital harm. So he has nothing to gain from his tax "premium."

This objection, though, puts the focus in the wrong place. It dwells upon the source of the condition and not the condition itself. If applied to welfare, it would admit aid only to those who fall into poverty, ignoring those born into poverty.

Of course, we do not have the technology to remove most congenital barriers. There are no such intelligence-boosting chemicals. But if there were, we should seek to provide them.

We must again qualify this policy. A people should have access to parks, dramatic productions, fine dinners, sporting events, advanced studies, and travel. These things should not vanish from the world, harming us all. So the state must take care to preserve them. When the tax burden is so great as to effectively eliminate culture, then it should be adjusted. This is reminiscent of triage. We may well find ourselves unable to tackle all injustice. Some people may have to forget air-traffic controlling. We may not be able to grant some freedoms. But in all this, we should try to provide the most freedom we can. That is to say, we should remove as many limitations as we can. The simple preservation of innocent life is crucial. Living wages and welfare support along the lines drawn in earlier discussions is obligatory, except in dire national circumstances. As we pursue our attack on the barriers, we find hard choices. Should we work at enhancing the mobility of the handicapped or preserving the vitality of the performing arts? Should we provide special vocational training for para- plegics or extend Amtrak service? A balanced attack on limitations is the special task of the statesman. Surely here it is fair to say that there are no easy answers.

Finally, something should be said about health care prices. In the section on prices, we saw that artificial controls on infinite things is damaging to our freedom. If, to pick up the analogy, someone or some group checks out the library book and then retains control of the knowledge and use of its processes, there is a harmful check. This sort of control can escalate prices, making access to the techniques more difficult than is necessary. The competition which checks this abuse is denied.

Insofar as this is the case for medical training and practice, there is injustice. Doctors deserve salaries that are a fair return for their many years of training and constant dedication their profession calls for. However, medical schools can provide a greater degree of fairness and justice to the populace by not limiting the number of doctors on an arbitrary basis. People will pay whatever is necessary for health care. But this fact doesn't mean that doctors deserve fees that go beyond what is fair. Doctor's work is vital, significant, and requires great effort. But the same goes for garbage collectors and soldiers. The structure of entitlement, not of desert, favors doctors.

Foreign Aid

Foreign aid programs are often like welfare to underdeveloped countries. We send them technology, food, and materials to help put or keep them on their feet. Obviously, there are millions of victims of one sort or another around the world. Floods, drought, overpopulation, and plague generate a long list of persons receiving undeserved harm. Unquestionably it is just to help these people. But there's a snag.

While justice names many projects or goals under the categories of caring for the sick and punishing offenders, we are not to do these things at any cost. If, in the pursuit of these aims, we find ourselves facing an unjust means, we should stop. We should do justice, but not unjustly. We have no warrant to kill wealthy landowners just to get their land for the poor. The end does not, as far as we're to judge, justify the means.

You will recall that taxing the nation for welfare is just because the taxpayers receive coverage for their money. They are protected in the event they themselves become victims. The loss of freedom they apparently suffer in the loss of money is returned in the form of "insurance." There is not a net loss of freedom to the taxpayer. If, however, the system does not protect some of the taxpayers, it is unjust. Their money is taken without a return. April 15 becomes just another stickup. Or it would have to be construed as a fine, as punishment for something. Of course, neither of these fit. Income tax enhances and secures our freedoms.

What of foreign aid? As bloodless as it may seem, any foreign aid which fails to give the taxpayer a return on his money is unjust to him. If, in the pursuit of worthy ends, the state takes money without increasing the "coverage," then justice is done unjustly. If I feed the poor by cutting your throat and raiding your pantry, I err. If I finance the Bangladesh court system by robbing strollers in New York's Central Park, I further the cause of justice unjustly. If I take one hundred dollars from you by threat of imprisonment and give that money to a sufferer whose restoration does not affect you, then you suffer net loss. You are harmed by my humanitarian efforts. So it is with foreign aid. If the money taken from taxpayers does not go in some way toward furthering their freedom, then it is unjust.

It is not enough that the money help genuine victims. If that help does not go toward our national interest, then it is inappropriate. This is not at all to say that humanitarian efforts directed toward other nations are wrong. The people are free to organize massive voluntary relief efforts on their own. And if they are sensitive, compassionate people, they will do this. But when the collection for relief becomes involuntary, then the donors are due a return.

Perhaps this sounds like a selfish stance to take toward the world: "I won't help unless I am helped." In some respects it is; some of the taxpayers who might begrudge foreign aid would only spend the money on frivolous things. But there are others who would channel the money into other charitable causes. By sending my money say to Bangladesh, the state makes me unable to send help to a poor Palestinian boy identified by my church's missionaries. State officials should be like investment brokers as they work with money which is not their own. To play fast and loose with others' money is less than admirable. The broker may well delight in pouring investors' money into desperate companies, but he is acting irresponsibly—even selfishly—in treating others' money in this fashion.

None of what I've said automatically rules out any sort of foreign aid we now give. It simply shows the form any argument for a specific aid program should take. It is just not enough to argue that people are hurting, and we have the resources to help. This does not make all foreign aid contractural; we don't always have to receive promises in writing in return for our aid. Our return may come more subtly. By feeding the drought victims of one country, we might prevent their invasion of a well-fed country, upsetting the balance of power in the region, threatening our security. Or by feeding those people, we present to the world an example of compassion and cooperation which infects other nations, making the world a safer place to live. National acts of compassion could serve to endow that nation with a moral authority in the eyes of the world; the judgments and security of the nation would be attacked only at the risk of worldwide disapproval and sanction. Whatever the return on foreign aid, it is always necessary that one be assumed.

War

Under this heading, we will consider several issues of public policy, the declaration of war, the actual conduct of the war, and the draft. As was the case for the other discussions, this one will be brief, sketching only general guidelines in accordance with the matrix.

A declaration of war commits the nation to enormous expenditure. It ties up large amounts of tax money. We saw earlier that unless this money goes toward "coverage" for the taxpayer, he suffers a net loss of freedom. If my money is taken for a cause unconnected to my own situation, then I am harmed. My range of choices is reduced. To avoid victimizing its citizens in this fashion, the state should examine such expenditure for its return to the taxpayer. This policy extends to war appropriations.

If the war is of no significance to the people of the warring nation, then it, at least, does them economic injustice. Consider, for example, the loathesome reign of Idi Amin in Uganda. There was a substantial stream of reports of atrocity under his rule. A church leader was assassinated on the highway; members of the political opposition were bludgeoned to death with sledge hammers; Amin himself is said to have literally tasted the blood of certain of his victims. Although it is hard to sort out fact from fiction, it is fairly clear that Amin was a murderous ruler whose policies were unjust. What was to keep us from sending in troops to depose him? Certainly there could have been satisfaction in that choice. But is this enough? No doubt the world is full of earnest causes—starving people, murderous rulers, political prisoners. But not every need is a call, so to speak. The state is not justified in being gracious with the money of its citizens unless they are helped themselves. If the continued rule of a tyrant poses no significant threat to the well-being of American citizens, then military intervention in his country is inappropriate, regardless of how disgusting he is.

There might, as we have seen, be room for the argument that every murderous ruler poses a threat to all of mankind and that no member of the family of nations can suffer without the entire family suffering. Here might be a way to justify intervention, but it does seem to be stretching the point a bit. A Soviet invasion of

Mexico could easily be construed as a threat worthy of some serious expenditure, but how exactly were we threatened by Amin?

It is unjust to take another's money to pay for something which does not help him. But war can involve an even more serious injustice to the citizen, for wars are not fought strictly with money and materiel; they require people. As so there is the matter of the draft. It is obvious how tax money can help the taxpayer, but what about a tax on a citizen's services? When a person is drafted, he is obligated to leave what he's doing, undergo rigorous training, and face risks—even death. This amounts to a fairly high tax. What return does he enjoy for his "investment"? What sort of coverage could possibly compensate for loss of life—a bugler at the funeral?

Our theory makes way for two arguments here, the first for a wartime draft, and the second for peacetime, military training conscription. The first is harder to make. If it is to succeed, it would need to take the following form.

To begin with, a declaration of war should not place a person in peril. It should be declared only when he is already in peril. If wars are waged only when the citizens are threatened, then they do not create an artificial threat themselves. Now it might be argued that the level of threat or peril is uneven. We, as a nation, might face tyranny. But can this loss of freedom warrant our own acts of killing and risk of life itself? Isn't there some truth to the old expression, "Better Red than dead"? How can I justly be "taxed" for risk of life when the threat is itself, when unopposed, not so grave? Wouldn't it be better to submit to the aggressors, thereby preserving our lives?

This sort of thinking underestimates the perils of life under an unjust government. For purposes of analogy, we might look to an aircraft hijacking. The hijackers may have no intention of killing the passengers. They merely make room for murder in the event their plans are frustrated in some way. To them life is cheap, but they won't kill without reason. If, though, a passenger decides to visit the bathroom in a tense moment, tries to get off the plane, yells objections to their policies, or resists a humiliating order, he may be shot. The passenger who behaves may get the feeling that all is secure for him. He willingly gives up his freedom of movement around the plane in exchange for his life. But he errs in thinking he is secure, for the next moment, the whim of the hijackers could leave him dying. They might decide to kill all Jews or South Africans aboard. They might issue an order to which, in his old age, he is unable to respond quickly enough. He may be selected at random to die in a demonstration of the hijackers' earnestness. Life under those willing to murder is indeed perilous. The threat, even for those willing to cooperate, is real.

This airplane situation matches the situation found in a number of nations around the world. When we are faced with what amounts to a hijacking ourselves, we may count the threat to life as genuine. The citizen who submits, in effect, presents the state with a permit to execute him when it pleases. By acquiescing to that sort of rule, the citizen is analogous to the appointee who files a letter of resignation with his employer on the day that he is hired. The employer always has the option of digging that letter out of the file and accepting the resignation. The murderous despot who enjoys the obedience of his subjects has a file full of death warrants signed by the potential victims themselves. The certificates are at his fingertips if the need arises.

Granting then that the peril is genuine, what return does the draftee enjoy on his investment? Oddly enough, security. His chances for survival are increased by his participation. Every addition to a rifle squad increases the chances that the squad will survive. The additional member contributes to the base of fire the squad can lay down to cover their maneuverings. This addition can provide the crucial margin of suppression which is essential to success. Each additional soldier in the defense increases the chances that all will live through the repulsion of an attack. In fact, if the numbers are substantial enough, the enemy may not attack at all. In short, my contribution increases the probability of a success of which I am the beneficiary. There are no guarantees that I will enjoy the fruits of my efforts, but there are no guarantees for me in their absence either. The citizen of a nation under threat is in trouble, whether he fights or not. If he fights, he acts to reduce the threat. He enjoys a return on his contribution to the extent that he is an effective soldier. The better his readiness, the greater his security.

This view rules out suicidal war. If the soldier has no hope of a return in the form of security on his investment, then he is being "taxed" unjustly. If, however, his service enhances the security of the nation, and if he has a reasonable hope of survival to enjoy that security, he is not unjustly taxed by the draft.

In organizing the draft, the state should aim at two mutually dependent goals—that the scheme achieve the maximum security for the state and for each individual. If the draft is keyed to the talents of the individual citizens, then each person will find himself strategically placed. Since his role is strategic, he will enhance the security of the state, a security he enjoys. In other words, an intelligent division of labor provides the best for everyone. This is, no doubt, an ideal, but one which is not so far removed that it becomes useless.

An infantryman on the line may well consider his security second rate in contrast with the security he would enjoy at a desk job in the rear, but this can be specious reasoning. He might wish for a job with a logistical computer center instead of with a rifle squad. But his ineptness at the computer work could queer the supply system, undermining the readiness of the line troops. And their vulnerability could imperil him. If he had stayed on the line, the healthy flow of supplies overseen by others could have supported a level of combat readiness which could deter enemy attack. This is obviously a self-serving, contrived case, but it can illustrate a good working principle. A just draft makes the best use of the human resources at hand. If the total scheme of service is effectively administered, the profit goes to citizens at all of the various stations.

Any scheme which ignores the range of talents and potential in the community is unjust. If the scheme is arbitrary or biased, then the people receive a weak return on their investment. If a favored group is exempted from service, without good cause, then the entire war effort is undermined by the loss. Their talents are lost, and others must be juggled to cover the gaps. This cut-and-paste approach to military organization makes for a weaker defense. Regardless of how nice his exemption might appear to him, the citizen places his state in jeopardy by his neglect and ultimately places himself in peril. The state whose draft policy permits these gaps is not a good steward of the power and money it administers. Its irresponsibility serves to deny appropriate coverage to those who pay for it.

The best minds in the country may, of course, play a more crucial role in time of war in the universities. Just as easily, they might serve best in the military. It might even be the case that the extraordinary demands of ground combat would require those with the quickest and most comprehensive judgment. It is conceivable that the nation would be best served by placing those with IQs over 150 in infantry companies. Whatever the decision, it should not honor considerations irrelevant to the security and well-being of the society.

There is, then, a chance that the state will cheat me by not sending me to the front lines. I have supported a selective-service system and a military structure, placing my trust in their will and capacity to provide security. My own participation in combat would serve to enhance that security. And yet I am exempted from this service. They have cheated me, paradoxical as it might seem. In the final analysis, I would have been safer on the line with a rifle than at home reading the paper.

None of this makes sense if the war is waged in the absence of national peril. If there is no serious threat to the citizens, those on the line are obviously in greater danger than those at home. Nobody who stays home is cheated. If men are drafted to fight in such a way, they are "taxed" without suitable coverage. The national security is not enhanced by their service. They give unnecessarily, and without recompense.

This completes the argument sketch for a wartime draft. Perhaps its standards are unworkably ideal. For it does seem that in virtually all wars, front-line soldiers face greater risks than the general populace.

It's not clear what a general nuclear exchange would do to this calculation. It might simply render all such figuring moot by making the role of military manpower negligible.

It does seem that just wartime draft is rare because it so often means more personal sacrifice than does surrender. Still, just wars may be fought by those who, uncoerced, offer their lives for the sake of the freedoms described in this book. And we may hope and even trust that volunteers will be available to serve such causes.

We should note and briefly reject one argument for wartime draft. Some say that I owe my life to my country's military service because others died for me, at Yorktown, at Normandy, and so on. Though this is personally stirring and compelling, it fails as moral proof. Very simply put I did not ask them to do this for me, and I cannot be morally bound by these unrequested services. I am not obliged to pay the man who mows my lawn without my asking. Even if he shields me from an assassin's bullet, I am not required to do the same for him if the situation arises. His act was supererogatory, beyond his call of duty, and reciprocal behavior is likewise beyond mine. It would be admirable for me to follow suit, but not a moral necessity.

So much for wartime draft. Peacetime draft, so long as it is for training, is much easier to justify. The deterrent effect of a capable force serves the nation nicely, and its cost does not include loss of life. The draftee gives up time, energy, and comfort, but he may reasonably suppose that the returns are generous.

Some may argue that unless this force is compelled to serve in time of war, the deterrent effect of the training is void. This is not so. A would-be invader plays a dangerous game of chance he would not otherwise face. He must bet that the host of trained men will not join together to meet him. If there is no host of trained men, prospects are less intimidating. The deterrent effect is real, so the draftee enjoys coverage for his tax.

The *lex talionis* does not apply to war in the same way it applies to internal criminal law. The matrix provides a model for the governance of a state. Officials of a state are instruments of justice; there is no world state. No one authority is in a position of sovereignty over all nations. Nobody bears the responsibility of feeding victims of all the world and punishing all the world's offenders. It is, of course, conceivable that such a sovereign exist. If he did, then he would be obliged to honor those responsibilities. He would be reprehensible in excusing offenders, for example. But as things stand, nobody has the duty to punish the murderers of other countries. It is inappropriate to wage a war strictly on the grounds of punishment. In the absence of world government, there is no place of an international *lex talionis*.

Despite the fact there is no duty to execute murderous people of other nations, it is permissible to kill in self-defense. Here the state is not acting as a world sovereign but as a wall against injustice to its own people. Its authority does extend to matters affecting its citizens. Economic strictures, inconveniences, and insults fail to justify war; but when the other nation is aggressive and homicidal, it is permissible. As with hijackers it is not necessary that they actually kill before they may be fought, for their project is clearly a threat to the lives of others. By brandishing arms they show their low regard for human life, and it is just to kill them preemptively.

Since the victorious nation stood in no position of world sovereignty, it has no obligation to punish all offenders at war's end. Prisoners of war do not have the same status as ordinary murderers, even though their war acts were murderous. Justice is not frustrated by their release since the demands of justice are limited to the state's treatment of its own. It might be in the best interests of the citizens of a state to punish prominent enemy leaders at war's end. Their continued freedom could spell new trouble, and their punishment could dissuade other national leaders from aggression. But the expression *war criminal* is specious in the absence of a world sovereign. It should not be used as a rationale for the execution of losing leaders or soldiers. The expression *criminal* is relative to the internal structure of a particular state.

A good deal has been written on just war theory and I find little to add. The key point I want to make in closing touches the conduct of the war. Earlier we saw the flaw in lesser-of-two-evils thinking. The principle "Do justice justly" was urged in opposition to a utilitarian approach. We must refuse to harm innocents in the pursuit of worthy ends, whether they concern national defense, health care, or welfare. Although it is just to defeat the enemy, that victory is not justly won unless innocents are recognized. But who are these innocents?

Those in the military may be held responsible for the war, as may those who support the effort on the home front. The man assembling a fragmentation grenade is as involved in the war effort as the soldier in the field. Armies and factories are suitable targets. Even docks and farms may be justly attacked because of their supportive role. War should stop short of killing those not capable of supporting the war effort. Small children cannot choose to war as their parents can, and a strong effort should be made to avoid harming them in the conduct of war. This means a policy of avoiding the destruction of population centers. Regardless of how dire the circumstances, the willful killing of infants is unjust. The nuclear bombing of Hiroshima and Nagasaki and the

fire bombing of Tokyo were unjust. This was utilitarian calculation at its worst. Justice should be done justly.

Public Education

Children do not deserve education; they've done nothing
exemplary or productive to warrant the investment it takes to
school them. So we must look elsewhere in the matrix for a
rationale if there is to be one. The category of the victim, as we
shall see, serves this purpose.

The uneducated child finds himself, when he knows and cares
enough to notice, at a distinct disadvantage. He lacks the skills
and information necessary to act effectively in the world. He is
ringed about with limitations. The bright potential he once
enjoyed is diminished. He has lost time in developing himself,
and his stores of energy are less than they once were. A road to a
full range of freedoms was blocked by the neglect of his parents
and society to provide a basic education. In the interest of
preventing the victimization of the child, we should publicly fund
education.

There are other potential victims. If the children are not
educated, the rest of us are put into a dangerous situation. Unless
parents have been scrupulous in raising their children, society
faces a flood of incompetent people. Without years of instruction
in the features of productive citizenship, the children are a threat
to our security. An illiterate, morally ambiguous, shortsighted
person is more than useless; he is dangerous. So public education
also serves to prevent the victimization of society.

The curriculum should address both forms of victimization. It
should, first of all, be education for citizenship. The child should
study government, geography, history, ethics, and logic. He
should learn to communicate effectively, to organize his time,
and to be aware of the consequences of his acts. He should learn
how his body works and the nature of the ecosystem. It is
important that he learn some basic things about God. Unless a
child learns these things, he is a liability to society. We are

harmed by the loss of freedom we face in coping with the defective citizen.

Education for citizenship helps not only society, but the child too. He, too, is victimized by its absence. But education should be more than this. It should present the full range of vocational and avocational alternatives open to the child, so that he can take steps toward developing his capacity to enjoy them. Music, athletics, business, drawing, politics, forestry—he needs to be made aware of these institutions before it is too late for him to effectively join in them. A professional musician, for instance, needs to get started before adulthood. In short, the child needs to learn his talents and options if he is to enjoy adulthood. We have a responsibility to avoid victimizing him by leaving his blinders on.

It is not necessary that education come in the form of a public school. So long as private schools serve the purposes named above, so long as they are not antithetical to the interests of the child and society, they may receive public funding. Regardless of who does the educating, justice demands that all children enjoy it. They do not deserve it, but none of us deserves the unhappy consequences of the alternative.

5
Case Law

While appellate judges rightfully and of necessity construct their opinions with reference to statute law and court precedent, there is room for the more direct counsel of justice in their work. *Riggs* vs. *Palmer* (22 N.E. 188) stands as a well-known example. Elmer Palmer murdered his grandfather so as to secure his inheritance. His attorneys argued that the will had been properly executed and that the letter of the law must be served. Justice Earl rejected this reasoning and appealed instead to common law. He wrote:

No one shall be permitted to profit by his own fraud, or to take advantage of his own wrong, or to found any claim upon his own iniquity, or to acquire property by his own crime. These maxims are dictated by public policy, have their foundation in universal law administered in all civilized countries, and have nowhere been superseded by statutes.

Here we get a taste of higher law, of universal standards, of basic moral norms. Although the judge tied his decision to common law, the principles emerging from the history of court practice, the tone of purely moral conviction is unmistakable. The law can and should make a place for this sort of sensitivity. Indeed, the common law is a sort of official version of the moral law.

The courts, then, do more than search for the law as it is. They also declare, with effect, what the law should be. I would hope that, in so doing, their positions would conform to those that follow.

De Funis vs. *Odegaard*
Supreme Court of Washington (1973)
(Reverse Discrimination)

Marco De Funis was denied admission to the University of Washington School of Law. It was his contention that, because of preferential treatment for minority applicants, less qualified students than he were admitted. This, he argued, was a violation of the equal protection guaranteed by the Fourteenth Amendment. He brought suit against the administrators of the University of Washington, asking the Superior Court to issue an order that he be admitted to the school. This court decided in his favor. But the Washington Supreme Court and the United States Supreme Court both rejected the original court's decision, and so De Funis was not admitted.

These higher courts argued, among other things, that this sort of racial discrimination could not be fairly compared to other, unjust forms since it did not stigmatize whites. Furthermore, LSAT scores alone do not adequately guide admissions—personal qualities, for example, should also count. Students in a virtually all-white school miss the experience of functioning in a pluralistic society. Finally, the desperate condition of racial minorities makes strong corrective action necessary. Society has a perfect right to take racial makeup into account in pursuing the common good.

Here is a case of what is popularly called reverse discrimination. Legislation effecting this policy goes under the name of affirmative action. Whatever the label, here is an effort to correct past injustices. It is undeniable that for many years blacks were denied many freedoms enjoyed by whites—access to restaurants, administrative jobs, schools, swimming pools, and hotels. The list could go on and on. The suppression of blacks was so thorough that they were unable to spring forward when the pressure was released. Generations of injustice had caused significant loss of capacity and confidence among blacks. The external limitations generated internal limitations. In short, blacks were not instantly ready to compete with a change in law. In the judgment of the state, extraordinary measures were required to put blacks on an equal footing with whites. The same sort of policy is now being extended to other groups who have experienced harmful discrimination in the past—Indians, Chicanos, women, and Chinese-Americans. Affirmative action, then, is a response to injustice. But is it a just one?

The original discrimination was unjust in that it constituted a genuine harm to innocents. Black persons were boxed in; their freedom was checked. They were denied available means of self-expression, of action. Their role-playing capacity was arbitrarily limited. It's not enough to say that they had their own facilities and jobs. Even if black schools had been as good as white schools, a black might not have wanted to attend one. Perhaps he would have seen more promise in mixing with whites during his school years; this could have better prepared him for life and work in a predominantly white society. But whatever the reason for his interest in attending a white school might have been, arbitrary policies prevented it.

Central to this whole discussion is the concept of relevant differences. Discrimination based upon these relevant differences is not unjust since the limitations belong to the person himself. They are not arbitrary, imposed limitations. I am not free to join the US Olympic track team because of relevant differences between its members and me. They are world-class runners, and I'm not. My inability to compete on a world stage is a personal matter, not a social injustice.

But what of DeFunis' case? Has his role-playing capacity been externally limited or reduced? It seems clear that it has. His access to a law school was not based strictly upon his capacity to study and practice law or his capacity to enrich the incoming class. To be sure, there might be several reasons to prefer a black to a white in admissions. A black could bring a new perspective to classroom discussion. He could help accustom the white students to working closely with minorities. Beyond law school, he could serve as an important servant to the minority community. In these respects, De Funis' exclusion could be just. He just doesn't fill the bill when you consider what the school wants to accomplish. To insist that these alone are the grounds for DeFunis' rejection would be somewhat dishonest. If there had been no state pressure to admit a certain proportion of blacks, DeFunis' chances would have been better. There was, in the admissions procedure, competition among blacks, but not between blacks and whites. The government's rationale was not so much that of fostering interracial understanding as correcting past injustices. In sum, De Funis' rejection was based in large measure upon irrelevant differences. His role-playing capacity was reduced not because of what he is or does but because of what his ancestors did. He is, in effect, punished for the sins of his fathers.

No doubt the equality of blacks with whites in our nation is a good thing. But the state approach of enforced discrimination is one of doing justice unjustly. Here is a good aim pursued in the wrong fashion. Innocents are harmed for the sake of a larger good. For reasons given earlier, this is unacceptable for public policy. You should not help innocents by harming innocents.

But how else can they be helped? There are solutions, but they take time. Society can make every effort to give black children a first-rate education; if they are behind, special attention can be given to them as it is to whites who are behind. The general public can be educated in the plight of blacks. A wealth of information could be disseminated to blacks, making clear the full range of opportunities now available to them. All these take time, but to rush ahead with an unjust plan is a mistake.

Reverse discrimination could generate long-lasting feelings of ill will among whites which could, in the last analysis, undermine integration and equal opportunity. It could subtly introduce new feelings of inferiority into the black psyche; they might come to think that their gains in the public sector are rigged and not based upon their worth. Perhaps reverse discrimination would set blacks up for failures which would only enforce old racist attitudes. Or maybe this exercise in unjust justice would foster other unjust policies. Whatever the reason, I believe that policies which harm innocents are more harmful to society than those which do not. I take this to be the teaching of a loving God and am confident that it is pertinent to human well-being.

The Supreme Court's decision, then, was, on my view, unjust. This is not, of course, to say that they were bad people. Rather, in this case they were mistaken. Reverse discrimination is unjust and not in our nation's best interests. Whether it favors Blacks, women, Chicanos, or even WASPS, reverse discrimination is wrong.

At this point it is appropriate to discuss hiring and admissions policies of Christian colleges. Many restrict admission and hiring to Christians of a particular sort. Often there are strict behavioral guidelines, touching a range of acts from smoking to homosexuality. Are these policies just?

There are two questions to consider: (1) Are the purposes of these schools just? (2) Is the discrimination relevant to these purposes? A general affirmative answer may be given to the first question. On the whole, these colleges are concerned with graduating whole and effective Christians who will serve their fellowman with love, wisdom, and skill. Some schools are better at this than others. Still, the answer is yes. As for the second question, a look at the various segments of a college is important. What would be true for faculty might not fit the staff.

The expression *integration of faith and learning* is commonplace on Christian college campuses. It signifies a family of practices designed to bring biblical perspectives to bear on scholarship with the conviction that all reality and so truth is under God's sovereignty. Secular learning can inform one's understanding of Scripture, while Scripture can inform one's work in an academic discipline. Consistency between the two is sought. Where there is apparent conflict, either Scripture is given a different interpretation or academic theory is rejected or modified. Underlying the enterprise is the principle that the truths of Scripture and the truths of other disciplines are parts of a single picture. This is the image the college believes the student must have to be a whole and effective Christian servant.

This sort of integration obviously demands Christian commitment and academic competence. Discrimination on either of these grounds is relevant. Since most people lack either the training, conviction, or will to pursue this aim, the positions requiring this sort of work are open to relatively few people. But there is no injustice in this.

The integrative task can be found in a wide range of disciplines. Philosophers integrate their study of justice with biblical perspectives. Psychologists bring their Christian notions of man into a study of behaviorism. Literature professors trace and comment on theological themes in fiction. Dramatists present spiritual truths and raise spiritual questions in a variety of productions. And so the practice of integration goes. But there are some disciplines in which the relevance of Christian commitment to employment is not as clear. How, for example, is the mathematician to bring the Bible to bear on his discipline? Isn't math untouched by theological considerations? Isn't the calculus above doctrinal furor? Bishop George Berkeley didn't think so. He considered the calculus' reference to infinitesimals a dangerous thing because of the impossibility of our framing an image of infinity. In other writing he took pains to show the importance of purely abstract ideas to the atheist's world view. So in the calculus he detected the grounds for atheism. Now Berkeley doesn't have to be correct in his thinking for my point to be made. There can be genuine controversy, and so study, about the connection between Christianity and mathematics. The nominalist/realist/conceptualist debate, so popular with medieval churchmen, also rears its head in mathematics. So integration is possible even here.

More than this, it is important to the mission of a Christian college that the faculty demonstrate a Christian life-style. Integration goes deeper than the propositions one affirms or denies. There is also a need to integrate one's Christianity with his approach to work. Ideally, the Christian math professor is zealous in his study and teaching, exhibits a spirit of loving servanthood, and shows a biblical sense of priority in his professional life. His form of life then is also instructional. So Christian colleges which insist upon academic excellence and Christian commitment in its faculty are acting justly. The purposes are just, and the discrimination is relevant to these purposes.

As for the students, it may also be important to restrict admission on the basis of Christian commitment. If the college aims to evangelize through its course of study and campus life, then it would need to admit non-Christians. But if its aim is to more finely tune Christians, it may be important to exclude non-Christians from enrollment. If, for example, the teacher aims to lead the aesthetics class in a Christian understanding of the role of the artist, his work would likely be disrupted by the basic challenges of an agnostic student. The student might ask why it is important to consider this question when Christianity is itself questionable. A Christian school forced to do a good deal of internal apologetics is sidetracked from the pursuit of the deeper questions of Christian life and thought. It helps, in many discussions, to be free to assume a basic level of agreement and understanding among the discussants. Since the aims of a nonevangelistic Christian school may be just, discrimination in admissions on the basis of Christian commitment may be just.

Discrimination in staff employment may pose a special difficulty. There are, of course, staff members who work closely with the students and whose contribution as role models could be important. Earnest Christian cashiers, student aid secretaries, painters, and postal clerks can, in the course of their work, exert a powerful influence upon the minds of students. They can demonstrate how one should live and work, and their comments could instruct as well as those of the professors. In contrast, the bitter or godless deportment of a staff member could poison the atmosphere that the college considers important to its particular sort of learning.

What harm would be done by an atheistic or homosexual typist? What is at stake here for the college? Imagine that our typist addresses envelopes, takes breaks only in the staff lounge, and refrains from pushing his life-style on the students. Would the college be hard pressed to make out a convincing case for discrimination in this instance? Would a court which ordered a stop to the demand that the position be filled by a Christian be unjust? Would such discrimination in hiring be close to if not guilty of unjust irrelevance? The college's case for discrimination might be made around the concept of "Christian team spirit." It might be argued that the effectiveness of the staff in their support of the educational aims of the college is dependent upon mutual, prayerful support among the staff. This approach might work, but it would be entirely fair for the state to place the burden of proof upon the school in this case. It should take more than distaste to exclude a whole class of applicants.

Buck vs. *Bell*
United States Supreme Court (1927)
(Sterilization of Retarded Persons)

Carrie Buck was classified as feebleminded and so committed to Virginia's State Colony for Epileptics and Feebleminded. Her mother, also feebleminded, was in the same institution. Carrie herself was mother of an illegitimate, feebleminded child. In accordance with an act of Virginia, approved in 1924, the Circuit Court of Amherst County ordered that Carrie's fallopian tubes be cut as an Act of Sterilization. The statute and court decision were based upon the principle that, under proper safeguards, sterilization was a proper step in protecting the health of the patient and the welfare of society. Upon appeal, the decision was affirmed both by the Supreme Court of Appeals of the State of Virginia and the United States Supreme Court. In delivering the supreme court's opinion, Justice O. W. Holmes wrote, "Three generations of imbeciles are enough."

Sterilization is, of course, a very serious matter. A particularly significant course of action, parenting, is closed off. Role-playing capacity is decreased, so there is genuine harm. If someone were to abduct, anesthetize, and sterilize you, a severe judgment would and should be brought against the assailant, for the damage is great.

But as we have seen in the discussion of welfare above, procreation is not strictly a personal matter, whether the law chooses to treat it as such or not. Even the birth of a healthy child to ideal parents has an impact upon society. He presents to us all a new set of needs—nutrition, space, protection—to which we must adjust. In allocating the resources common to us all, we must take into account a new recipient.

When either the child or the parents have special problems, the effect upon society is magnified. If, for example, the child is seriously handicapped, requiring expensive educational techniques, the state may well be called upon for a measure of support in the interest of preventing the victimization of the child. Support, too, should be given to the children of welfare recipients. Unless help comes, these children of victims will themselves be victimized. Regardless of the imposition, no child should become a victim; for whatever need he presents to society is not of his own choosing. Justice demands that we care for all children. To make exceptions would be to tolerate undeserved harm, injustice.

The cost of a new child to society may be high. If its entire care falls upon us, we face a bill in the tens of thousands of dollars. Food, health care, and education for an entire childhood and youth is expensive. We might imagine some children as coming into the world with a bill in their hands, a bill we all must pay. But I do not say this to initiate a cost/benefit analysis of the life of a child. This point has no bearing here on the questions of abortion and infanticide. Regardless of the cost, you do not victimize another.

Instead, our attention should fall upon the parents. Culpability will be found here, if at all. Now I have pointed out that welfare should cover a measure of procreation; genuine victims should be helped in their choice to have families. Circumstance should no more deny them children than nutrition or freedom of movement. Parenting is so basic a part of the human enterprise that to deprive others of it by our tightfistedness would be a harm. But our commitment to make this option available need not be open-ended. So long as parenting at a reasonable level is open to indigents, we have prevented genuine victimization in this respect. No injustice occurs if we accept responsibility for only a few children. If the indigent has more than a few at our expense, then his extravagance is unacceptable. We are supporting wants rather than needs, and sanctions are due. These have been treated earlier.

What about sterilization rather than "fines"? Wouldn't this solve the problem more neatly? Yes, but neatness is not the ultimate criterion. Sterilization is terrifying in its finality. With a cut of the knife, a central human potential is gone. But hasn't the welfare mother's irresponsible behavior in bearing a fifth child earned her punishment? After all, her selfishness or negligence has penalized us tens of thousands of dollars. Imagine society's giving other people the right to do twenty-thousand dollars' damage at will, meekly picking up the bill after each binge. Isn't this, in effect, what procreating welfare recipients are forcing us to do? Procreate irresponsibly, and your ability to procreate is taken away. Isn't this a workable application of the *lex talionis*?

I would resist this approach on several grounds—the severity, permanence, and spectacle of the punishment, and the chance that the harm to society can be remedied otherwise. My answer for indigents appears in the previous chapter. It takes into account the possibility of repaying society for its extra support.

But there are significant differences between the indigent and the mentally retarded person. While the indigent has the capacity to parent, the retarded person faces a natural limitation. He is incompetent to raise a child without victimizing him. Nature, not society, has limited his freedom to parent. It is no more our responsibility to underwrite his parenting than it is to provide driving opportunities for the blind. Not only are these people incapable of raising children themselves; they are also incapable of repaying society for the costs they've imposed through procreation. When retarded persons procreate, it is likely that their children would become wards of the state. If the children are also retarded, their wardship is usually permanent. Neither they nor their parents are or will be in a position to provide support.

So with the retarded, we would suffer the costs of their procreation without preserving or enhancing their personhood. Because of their makeup, child-raising is not among the options for the retarded. Sterilization removes nothing but the experience of pregnancy and birth. And it would not do to argue that this is essential to personhood.

In sum, for those who naturally lack the capacity to raise children, there is no right to procreate. We need not foot the bill for their pleasure. Indeed, we may well be doing them a favor by sparing them the imposition of a pregnancy whose fruits they cannot responsibly enjoy. Sterilization in such cases constitutes no harm, results in no loss of freedom, and so is not unjust.

While Holmes' ruling is, in principle, correct, recent newspaper articles have shown that he may have been mistaken in this particular case. Carrie's daughter, the third generation "imbecile," was considered a "bright child" by her second-grade teachers before she died of measles at the age of seven. Carrie and her sister Doris, both sterilized, went on to marry and live reasonably effective lives in Virginia communities. Until recently, Doris thought her inability to bear children was her own fault. She was originally told that her abdominal scar was a result of "an appendectomy and rupture."

These revelations cast a shadow on both the ruling and the practice in general. We are chilled by prospects of an unbridled eugenics program and humbled when we consider our own fallibility. But the moral of the story is caution, not prohibition. Grave errors do not serve as grounds for abolishing the criminal justice system. Neither should they here. Our attention to safeguards must be as keen as our attention to due process in the courts. I do not argue that every sterilization performed is warranted, just that there is a way to warrant one.

All this talk of sterilization is in no way meant to suggest the destruction of retarded persons. For they are persons indeed. And we should not harm innocent persons. But we no more harm the retarded by sterilization than we harm the congenitally blind by refusing them driver's licenses. Neither can handle the responsibility, and both should be kept from doing damage where there is nothing for them to gain. Sterilization is not a form of punishment for the retarded person; it is morally analogous to taking matches away from a child.

Paris Adult Theatre vs. *Slaton (District Attorney)*
United States Supreme Court (1973)
(Pornography)

Two Atlanta "adult" theaters were brought to trial on grounds of obscenity in violation of Georgia law. Criminal investigators for the local state district attorney bought tickets to two films, *Magic Mirror* and *It All Comes Out in the End,* and the civil action began. The trial court granted the obscenity of the films but dismissed the complaints because the theaters had taken the proper precautions that minors and unsuspecting adults not be exposed to them. The Georgia Supreme Court unanimously reversed this decision. The theater owners appealed to the United States Supreme Court, who supported the Georgia Supreme Court Decision. Justice Burgher wrote the majority opinion which essentially held that the First Amendment does not protect obscenity. He argued that it is reasonable to suppose that pornography has harmful effects upon society and that there is a significant state interest that it be regulated. Justices Douglas, Brennen, Stewart, and Marshall dissented.

The images of pornography are false and seductive. They can encourage improper attitudes toward sex and the family. Those who fall or place themselves under the influence of pornographic values may well become less fit for the roles of spouse and sibling in Christ. And while the effect of pornography is not so quickly and surely harmful as that of alcohol upon a driver, its disruptive, retarding, and degenerative influence can be found in many cases.

So should it clearly be illegal? One has only to think for a moment to realize that the culture is full of similarly dangerous ideas and images whose legality we would earnestly defend.

Take, for openers, the claim that there is no God. We Christians believe that this is a personally and socially destructive opinion. Those who hold to it are ill-equipped for the Judgment and the quality of their public lives can suffer. Whether at work in business, the home, politics, the arts, or the military, the person who rejects the notion of God may well prove less worthy on account of that rejection. Of course, there are nonbelievers whose lives and service are honorable, but there are countless cases of social harm which can be traced to godlessness.

Nevertheless, we Baptists, among others, defend a person's right both to reject God and to urge others to join in that rejection. Roger Williams made room for atheists in a day when it was dangerous to be so radical as to insist upon believer's baptism. God has given persons choices. When we allow persons to be atheists, we are honoring a freedom God has given persons. God himself doesn't violate this freedom. Therefore, we shouldn't.

Do we give some credence to atheism when we protect its legality? Not at all. We simply feel that people should not be forced by the state to abandon harmful and false impressions. We choose rather to work by prayer, persuasion, and example.

Returning to the matrix, we find the category, fool. He is one who believes and acts self-ruinously. God has given him leeway to "work out his own damnation," to be a fool, and it is appropriate for a society to grant the same privilege.

But don't fools harm others as well? Many do, and when they do, they become offenders. Offenders warrant punishment. This should be clear from the earlier discussion. But until the public harm or danger is "clear and present," they must be left alone. If an atheist embezzles funds as a result of his godless convictions, he should be punished. But he is not punished for his godless convictions. If a pornography enthusiast becomes a sex offender, he should be punished. But he is not punished for his involvement with pornography. And if a "mystic" becomes a mass killer because he hears "messages from God," he should be punished. But he is not punished because he awaits and receives "messages from God." Public harm rather than folly is the basis for punishment.

But have we construed public harm too narrowly? By focusing on sex offenders, have we missed the more substantial harm, societal rot? After all, pornography's opponents do not charge that the material typically drives its consumers into dangerous frenzy or criminal intrigue. They argue, rather, that the harm is insidious, long-range, and incremental. It serves over the years to confuse and deceive, to stunt the growth of, or displace healthier attitudes toward sex and humanity. Callouses form on the conscience, and the disciple of pornography comes to misperceive the God-ordained structure of human sexual well-being. Perhaps then we should take steps to eliminate pornography from the marketplace, lest we become a debilitated and irresponsible people.

Shall we, however, prohibit ideas, images, and practices which gradually undermine society? Consider the long-range effects of these notions: "It makes no difference what you believe as long as you're sincere"; "Might makes right"; "The end justifies the means"; "Religion is the opiate of the masses"; "Above all, look out for number one."

Consider, too, the marriage-threatening advice of radical feminists and radical masculinists, the advertiser's jolly picture of alcohol consumption, the crippling advice that maladjusted parents give their children, and the bubble-headed life-styles prescribed on talk shows. These and countless other impressions compete for and shape our commitment. So the threat of societal rot is far from unique to pornography. The crusader who seeks to marshall state forces to stamp out socially ruinous ideas and images not only tries to deny the fool his rightful freedom, but also cuts out for himself an impossible task. Further, this may be beyond the ability and the warrant of government.

Christians who wish to operate within the bounds of justice could choose better strategies against pornography. Pastors and laymen should speak, write, and preach persuasively on these matters, exploding false impressions and presenting Christian alternatives. Prayer is certainly appropriate. Parents should so exemplify and espouse Christian principles that the specious ideals of pornography will fail to capture their children. A bit of Christian imagination and love can generate some remarkable approaches to the problem. For example, a congregation might help the family of a jailed pornographer through an emergency. By providing them with care while the father is unable to see to it himself, they might well astonish, disarm, and convert him through their charity. Perhaps, too, a Christian businessman could offer the clerk of a pornographic shop an employment alternative, thereby working the owner of the pornography shop a hardship and providing the employee a way out of his circumstance. The "foolishness" of Christian love is a formidable weapon. And, of course, if the church can persuade the citizens that a diet of pornography is unnecessary and unhealthy, the pornographer may simply fail to turn a profit.

When Christians seek to outlaw pornography, they may allow the pornographer to change the subject to his advantage. Whereas, before, he was merely the champion of pornography, he may now appear to be the champion of civil liberty, of freedom. The latter cause is far more noble than the former, and we err if we allow him to play this role. He finds allies he never would have had and enjoys a higher, more principled, status than he could ever have hoped to enjoy in the absence of legal attack.

This is not to say that the community is obliged to give pornographers whatever they please. Certainly it is just to zone them from certain neighborhoods. Justice does not demand that a trucking firm shall set up wherever it pleases. For it is proper to preserve the freedom to enjoy a pleasant residential neighborhood. If the law allows pornography to exist, pornographers may still be restricted to certain districts for the sake of community tone.

Child pornography is especially inexcusable. Until a human being reaches an age of responsibility where society must grant him the right to become a self-ruinous fool, he is guarded. Just as a child may be compelled by his parents to attend church, while an adult may not, there are special guidelines for children in the sexual realm. Those who ignore these special immunities and restrictions should be punished.

Those Christians who would rid society of dangerous images and institutions would do well to watch lest they be attacked with their own strategies. What if the churches were to be held responsible for the malcontents they spawned? Would they welcome a government study of the link between religious belief and suicide? And what of the legislator who wants to do something about the fact that many political assassins have religious backgrounds or the powerful reformer who proclaims clear correlation between membership in a certain denomination and low reading scores?

The prospects are outrageous and alarming. We would, in part, object that churches are too varied, people too quirky, and other forces too numerous for anyone to lay clear blame for social harm on the churches. Besides, we would argue, churches don't force people to believe; people take what they will from them.

We should, therefore, be cautious in marshaling causal arguments against other institutions in the interest of censorship. If the cause of freedom for the other party does not satisfy us, perhaps the fear of turned tables will.

Was the decision of the Supreme Court unjust? A just society is one which safeguards human choosing—even if those choices are foolish. But how can a theory of justice, supposedly keyed to Scripture, allow pornography? How can we make use of the Israelite example in some instances while, in this case, ignoring the fact that obscenity was not tolerated among them? The answer calls for a recognition of mission and circumstance. Their's was not an ordinary society, one whose patterns and structures are suitable in all respects for contemporary use. Their mission was crucial and unique, and so were many of their rules. Their historical task and role called for special instruction, special purity, special discipline, and special attention. It is our job to distinguish those special, circumstantial rules from those more suitable for enduring use. In my judgment, my comments on *Paris Adult Theater* vs. *Slaton* honor the more universal and lasting principles of just government.

Nader vs. *General Motors Corporation*
Court of Appeals of New York (1970)
(Invasion of Privacy)

Ralph Nader, the consumer advocate, sued GM for invading his privacy, intentionally inflicting severe emotional distress, and interfering with his economic advantage. The conflict arose over Nader's book *Unsafe at Any Speed* which questioned GM's attention to safety in the design of automobiles.

When GM learned of the book's imminent publication, it began an effort to compromise or suppress Nader's cause through the use of damaging personal information. The corporation hired three men to build a case against Nader's integrity.

Nader claimed that GM had committed the following offenses:

(1) Interviews with his acquaintances over the most intimate matters;
(2) Unreasonable surveillance in public places;
(3) Attempts at entrapment with call girls;
(4) Threatening, harassing, and obnoxious phone calls;
(5) Wiretapping and electronic eavesdropping;
(6) Continuing and harrassing investigation.

GM, in turn, moved the dismissal of several of the charges; the Supreme Court, Special Term, New York County, denied this motion. Upon appeal, the New York Supreme Court, Appellate Division, affirmed the lower court's refusal to dismiss the charges. GM then took its motion to the Court of Appeals of New York. In the opinion cited above, the court determined which charges could count, if proven, against the defendant, and in what ways they could count. This was not to say that GM was actually guilty of those offenses; that was for the trial court to determine. The findings simply meant that, of the charges, only certain ones, if established, could damage the defendant. The others, even if supported by evidence, were insufficiently serious to warrant penalty.

The court reasoned that neither interviews, phone calls, nor entrapment attempts constitute invasion of privacy, in that mere annoyance is not an intrusion into private and confidential matters. When I confide in friends, I assume the risk that that confidence will be broken. Neither the accosting prostitute nor the telephone pest gain more personal information than I choose to reveal. Wiretapping, though, is a different matter; it is a sufficient basis for trial. The prostitutes, phone calls, etc. can count toward a different charge, the intentional infliction of severe emotional distress.

As for the economic interference charge, the court was less forceful, though open to further consideration. Nader charged that those watching him stuck so close that they were able to observe the number and denomination of the bills he withdrew from the bank. That sort of economic knowledge could undermine whatever business or investment strategies he might plan. While recognizing that bank withdrawals are made in public, the court stated the principle that "a person does not automatically make public everything he does merely by being in a public place." And so the bank surveillance charge was counted pertinent.

Why should a decent man care whether he is under surveillance? He has nothing to hide. Only criminals and other obnoxious characters stand to lose from this sort of scrutiny. In fact, these lower types prosper in the absence of surveillance. By putting strict safeguards on privacy we ensure that criminals will enjoy a low level of state interference. If, on the other hand, we were to open the way for eavesdropping, there would be a greater stock of information for us all to work with. Isn't it important that we have as many facts as we can in order to make intelligent decisions? What do I care if government agents tap my phone? I'm not involved in anything dishonest. So what if they were to discover that I regularly deceive the IRS? Wouldn't I deserve to be caught and punished? And who knows but that GM will turn up some important, damaging information on Nader. Wouldn't we want to know if Chrysler was funding his investigation of the Corvair? In short, what harm is there is invading another's privacy? Or, for our purposes, what undeserved harm is there?

Clearly, the crook can be harmed by our discoveries.

Consider the "peeping Tom." His eyes emit no damaging laser beams. How does his peering at me constitute a harm? It is highly unlikely that he will see anything surprising. Anyone who cares to think about it knows basically what I do in my bedroom and bathroom and how I appear undressed. The "Tom" only picks up a few of the specifics. So what? Why should the police bother to chase him down and charge him with an offense? Are they protecting me from the suffering I would face if people were to discover that I use the bathroom? What's at stake here? Why is privacy so important?

To begin with, there are the dangers of misinformation and of abuse of information. An eavesdropper may misconstrue what he observes; and since I am not aware of him, I cannot guide his perceptions. I lose the capacity to qualify, frame, or interpret what he sees. So I can be haunted by a stock of misinformation with which I am not familiar. This concern has led lawmakers to grant people access to their own credit, employment, and academic reference files. Perhaps this sort of law neutralizes the misinformation objection.

But isn't there another danger, that the state will misuse these files? It is conceivable that those opposing the incumbent party would suffer a slowdown in state services. Perhaps these incumbents could make use of embarrassing information in coercing opponents to soften their political activities. Virtually all of us have something we prefer not to share publicly. If the state's surveillance were so thorough that these details regularly found their way into the central data bank, then those in power could manipulate us as though we were marionettes. We're all familiar with the spectre of Big Brother.

But this hardly seems sufficient grounds for stringent privacy protection. For there are dangers in all cases where we grant state power. We equip the military with weapons which can blast through a tank's hull. Police have high-powered and automatic weapons, sophisticated night vision devices, and elaborate communications networks. There is both the possibility and reality of abuse, but we consider it important to so equip them. Their use of these things is subject to sanctions. They aren't entitled to use an anti-tank weapon to blow speeders off the highways. Neither may they use their electronic equipment to assist Mafia operations. The checks are there, and they might be for the use of information gained by surveillance. As strong as this abuse case may be, it still focuses upon what could happen through invasion of privacy and not what does happen. Since it is concerned with dangers rather than actual harms, precautions rather than prohibitions seem in order. With suitable safeguards we can enjoy the benefits of detailed information.

There is, however, a more fundamental problem with surveillance. It strikes at the very heart of personhood. As a person, an agent, I have a variety of programs, plans, strategies, missions, or ministries. I focus my energies accordingly. I do not chase after every possibility, for this would mean a diffuse life. On the contrary, I save up my resources, gather my forces, and move when it is appropriate to move. Essential to effective action is the chance to rest or recoup. I need a time for preparation, recreation, and relaxation. I need privacy.

When we are with others, we are conscious of their needs and opinions. We are concerned that their estimation of us will be altered by something we say or do. As long as they are there we are conscious of making a sort of presentation to them. We are "on stage." This last expression fits nicely with a drama analogy. Imagine that we present a romantic play with a transparent backdrop. The actors embrace and exit upstage only to drift apart to study lines and smoke offstage. We see them at their leisure and then watch as they drop their scripts, straighten their costumes, and return to stage for another romantic interlude. But the romance has lost its force. The offstage images distract us, and the play is done for. For the play to be effective, the actors must be genuinely offstage when they exit. They must carefully control how they present themselves if their charcters are to be persuasive.

There is, of course, an unfortunate way to take this analogy. It may be taken to suggest that our public behavior is merely an act, unsupported by our private behavior. We are fakes whose private moments could reveal our hypocrisy. Instead of protecting this privacy, we should open up our lives to careful scrutiny, exposing our humanity, foibles, or whatever. But let me suggest a more helpful reading. Serious personhood involves strategic presentation of ourselves. If we are earnest about values and their correlative actions, we will not squander our resources but channel them into our chosen projects. We will not allow ourselves to be constantly on stage because this would dissipate our powers. We would burn out. We know we must reserve time to drop out of character, to rest our faces, to breathe slowly, to be unresponsive and even unattractive. This does not reveal hypocrisy or sham but stewardship. We are practicing an economy of self-preservation; we withdraw for later effective presentation.

If my privacy is not protected, if I am not given control over my presentation, then my personhood is undermined. If I am never sure of my privacy, then I must always act as though I am being watched. That is to say, I must always play my role lest my message or project be undermined. This way of life cannot be maintained without serious damage. Privacy is essential to the preservation, the conservation, of personhood.

There is a curious notion that the private self is the real self. One of the questions of our day is "What's Johnny Carson really like?" When we find that he listens to jazz at home, studies astronomy, and plays tennis, we feel that we're really onto something. Might we not just as well count those off-camera roles as supporting while regarding the televised persona as genuine? Which serves which? Of course, a peek into a private life can reveal hypocrisy and fraud, but we tend to overrate these insights. At least equally important are the insights we gain from public observation. Here is where the person makes his stand. Here he shows his colors as he would have us understand them. He is known, in large measure, by how he presents himself. He is, in large measure, those concerns that he presents publicly. It is these that we must not neutralize by invading his privacy.

The court then was correct in ruling that wiretapping is a prosecutable offense. We must be protected from the threat of surveillance in the absence of "probable cause." Our personhood is at stake.

Kaimowitz vs. *Dept. of Mental Health for the State of Michigan*
State of Michigan in the Circuit Court for the County of Wayne (1973) (Psychosurgery)

Gabe Kaimowitz, working with the Wayne State University Law School legal services program, brought suit on behalf of Louis Smith, an involuntarily-held patient of the Michigan mental health system. Smith's detention was due to his raping and murdering a student nurse at the Kalamazoo State Hospital while he was there as a mental patient. Smith was sent to the Ionia State Hospital where he stayed until doctors at the Lafayette Clinic, also part of the state system, secured his transfer to their control for purposes of experimentation. Smith signed a statement agreeing to serve as a subject in a "study of treatment of uncontrollable aggression." The experiment involved the implantation of electrical wires in the brain for exploratory stimulation. If a connection between certain parts of the brain and aggression could be established, then electrical destruction of the problem areas would follow. Smith claimed that he wanted to be helped in this way.

When Kaimowitz heard of this, he brought civil action to block the experiment. In the early going, the court decided that Smith was being illegally detained. There was, they held, sufficient evidence of his ability to reenter society; and he was released. After determining that, despite his release, the issue of experimental psychosurgery was not then moot, the court looked into the practice. The aim was to issue a declaratory judgment affecting future practice.

There were two principle findings in support of Kaimowitz's cause:

(1) The informal consent of involuntarily-held patients should not count. Their judgment is suspect because of the threat of personality changes brought about by institutionalization. Such patients can, so to speak, lose their bearings and their sense of self-worth. Furthermore, the hope of release can lead them to make decisions they ordinarily would not make. In short, the atmosphere is coercive, and so informed consent is not genuinely voluntary.

(2) Whether or not the consent is informed and voluntary, experimental psychosurgery is not permissible. The state of the art is such that, with the control of aggression, there is also great danger that creativity will diminish. Patients often suffer "side effects" which make them less able to "generate new ideas." This is, then, a violation of the First Amendment principle of freedom of speech. The Constitution cannot allow a person to undermine his own freedom of speech unless it serves an overriding public interest. This was not the case with Louis Smith.

Psychosurgery directly and often irrevocably alters a person. Its effect makes the effects of theft, unemployment, discrimination, and censorship seem tame or even negligible. For there is an intimacy between a person and his brain not found even between him and his property, job, or entertainment. The gravity of mutilating a part of his cerebrum is unmatched by other offenses. With the slice of a surgeon's knife, I can be transformed into a radically different person. Can justice permit this?

It is obviously unjust to cut upon the brain of an innocent person against his will. The harm is so great as to rival the killing of that person. Even when the victim survives the action, his old self—his old personality—is, to a greater or lesser extent, gone. The structure of values definitive of his personhood is broken down or changed in a few minutes. He has no secret place in his mind where he can resist the forces of external circumstance. Rather, the circumstances are that that secret place has been directly violated.

On the other hand, there could be justification for psychosurgery as a form of punishment. This is a hard saying, but one that follows from the *lex talionis*. This principle no more makes room for psychosurgery as a preventive measure than it provides for precautionary imprisonment of children who have been raised badly. Just punishment is administered upon the basis of an actual offense and not simply potential. Indeed, preventive psychosurgery would not count as punishment at all, but there is a situation in which it would so count. If a person were to intentionally neutralize or alter another's brain surgically, pharmacologically, or violently, then he would deserve equal treatment. For eliminating another's personality he would deserve the elimination of his own personality. The punishment, though stiff, is no stiffer than the offense it answers. Of course, the penalty could be translated into another mode, imprisonment, for example. But the demand for proportional harm remains.

Of course, one could argue that psychosurgery can do more good than harm. Nasty people can become amiable. Surely this is a benefit. Freed from the tyranny of his former inclinations, the man can address life with new vigor and confidence. So how can we call all compulsory psychosurgery an injustice? Doesn't it depend on the case?

This argument proceeds as though we simply improve the

person undergoing surgery. But this is not the best way to put it. For the surgery erases or replaces the former self. The new person is nicer than the old person, and this is fine. It is not acceptable, however, to achieve fine things in just any fashion whatsoever. In this instance the means are wrong. In seeking a good end we take away freedom, the freedom of the former self to order his life as he sees fit. We may punish him for acts of aggression but not erase him purely for aggressiveness.

So much for psychosurgery on unwilling innocents and upon offenders. There remains another category—voluntary patients. Should a person be allowed to choose psychosurgery for himself? Is there injustice in this? The court ruled that self-harm is not an open-ended constitutional right. After all, they reason, it would be inconsistent to protect a person's freedom of speech while allowing him to dispose of it himself. The same sort of principle seems to be at work in the face of suicide attempts. Forlorn and desperate people are snatched from bridges, caught in cleverly concealed nets, and placed in padded environments. Whether the rationale is the preservation of free speech or the salvation of the true person from his own dark irrationality, the effect is the same. Citizens are kept from radical self-harm.

On the face of it, this policy denies freedom. The choice of leaving this world or of withdrawing from effective citizenship is proscribed. On the model we are using this counts as a harm, but there comes an obvious retort. By prohibiting suicide and voluntary psychosurgery, we do not reduce personhood and agency; instead, we ensure the continued possibility of it. What seems to be a denial of choice is, in fact, the preservation of choice. This claim is reminiscent of the earlier discussion of taxation. What seemed on the surface to be a harmful practice—taking a citizen's money—was shown to be on balance, helpful. The tax money goes to enhance the security and freedom of the citizen who pays it. There is net gain. The same sort of point was made about compulsory military service. We might call this the "net gain argument" for prohibiting self-harm.

While there are obvious similarities between taxation and intrusive rescue, there is a crucial difference. The benefits of taxation are desired while the benefits of rescue are repudiated. Naturally there are those who resent taxation. But these people do not reject the military defense, highways, and court structure their money provides. While they may resent the benefits going to indigents, they would welcome similar help if they became genuinely destitute. They may not believe that they receive a net gain on their tax investment, but they do not deny that they desire the sorts of goods at issue. The suicidal person, though, considers the "gains" you offer him through rescue and rejects them. He is not resentful because you give him too little. He is resentful because you give him any at all. He has arrived at the point of counting the gains and freedoms of life unsatisfactory. He has concluded that the earthly exercise of will no longer holds promise, if ever it did. The freedom you offer him no longer counts in his estimation. While taxpayers desire services, and draftees desire security, suicidal persons do not desire the freedom that life brings. What goes for suicide goes for other sorts of self-harm. If you take away my drugs or prohibit psychosurgery, you can give me something I don't want.

Often, the person who sets out to harm himself suffers from a passing delusion. He feels that nobody cares for him, that there is no hope of finding a meaningful vocation, or that he lacks the resources to go on after the death of his spouse. It is here that rescue may deliver net gain. In helping him we give him time to reconsider and an example of the regard we have for his well-being. It's not uncommon for the subject of enforced rescue to thank his rescuers for their interference. But this should not be the last word on the matter.

There is, in contrast, a studied and deliberate sort of suicide. The person, after taking into account the pattern and promise of life, decides that whatever death may bring will likely be an improvement. This judgment, though it may be wrong, is free and considered. At this point, it is unjust to interfere, because to persist in the name of freedom and personhood would be to do justice unjustly. The man has rejected the highest good the state can give him, freedom. He should be allowed to, so to speak, resign.

While the "net-gain" argument fails, there might be another case for proscribing self-harm. In the taxation section, I mentioned the debt that the taxpayer already has to the state. Whether he chooses it or not, the citizen is protected by a standing army and a police force. He profits from the work of the FAA, ICC, and FDA. So he is not free simply to exempt himself from taxation and its benefits. He is an automatic beneficiary.

Could the same be said for the suicidal person? Might not society demand that he remain in their midst, serving as he has been served? It might be argued that suicide leaves an unpaid debt, that his death rules out his ongoing contribution to the public good. While we ordinarily feel remorse over suicide or drug addiction, there is room for indignation as well. Someone has, in effect, checked out without fully paying his bill, but to translate this indignation into a prohibition would be wrongheaded. However high and perceptive our debt claim may be, it is a simple fact that people in a self-destructive state are generally incapable of making a contribution to the common good. On the contrary, their continued existence is ordinarily a drain upon the public. They often require the attention of support services—therapy, medical care, social work, police time. The responsible state, the state which is a genuine steward of the taxpayers' money, writes off this lost service as a bad debt. To insist upon "payment" by preserving the life and safety of the self-destructive person is to incur an even greater loss of resources. In principle, the suicide victim may be leaving without paying in full; but in practice it would be folly to retain him in order to get that payment. This is true as well of drug addicts, masochists, and lobotomy seekers.

In sum, a just state permits citizens to harm or kill themselves. In doing so it is honoring the choicemaking capacity God has given persons. Indeed, self-harm is not different in kind from other attempts to find an acceptable life-style. People everywhere are seeking the best forms of action to bring satisfaction or release from pain. The self-destructive courses of action are for the same ends. The court erred in prohibiting voluntary, dangerous psychosurgery. What sense would there be to freedom without the option to ruin oneself in a wide variety of ways?

A legal right to harm yourself does not carry with it a legal right to be cared for in your new condition. Public assistance is designed for victims, innocents. If you render yourself inert by elective psychosurgery or drug abuse, then you have a personal problem. Many argue that these people have succumbed to enormous pressures and so are victims, unfortunates. The scriptural policy does not honor these arguments. It cuts through psychological and sociological subtleties with a strong doctrine of personal responsibility. Whether or not this doctrine is based upon the most libertarian account of man is irrelevant. Whatever man's makeup, when he, as an adult, makes a conscious choice, he is to be regarded as if he were responsible. The biblical policy demands accountability. This is not to say that care should be denied in the private domain as well. Charity toward fools is praiseworthy here, but it would be unjust of the state to use public money for this purpose.

Louis Smith was chosen for inclusion in a "study of treatment of uncontrollable aggression." Surely his problem went beyond those of the ordinary unfortunate. While it is incorrect to excuse the offenses of the person whose behavior has been shaped by an oppressive or misguided upbringing, there does seem to be special cause to excuse the subject of uncontrollable aggression. The very expression rules out the exercise of will and denies the involvement of the person's value structure. The person who suffers from uncontrollable aggression is apparently "along for the ride" when his body attacks another. Can we make sense of this classification?

We might ask first whether the person is periodically taken by a sweeping delusion. Does he, for example, come to consider attending nurses as involved in a plot on his life? If so, then his assault is in self-defense. It's not at all clear what delusion could excuse Smith's ensuing act of rape. Indeed, the rape in the case at hand effectively removes the plea of delusion. While there might be a case for calling sincere acts of self-defense uncontrollable— that is, we cannot help but defend ourselves if we are normal— there seems to be no application here.

There is perhaps another way to excuse aggression. If the offender watches in horror as an alien spirit appropriates his body for its own evil purposes, he could be excused. This would fit with the biblical account of demon possession. Scripture does make room for the sudden and insidious displacement of a personality by another. The demon comes to control the life of the body during its tenure. There is a new person in charge, and this person's character can be read in the patterns of behavior he chooses. While there are reports of just such phenomena, their occurrence is rare and fantastic. Once again, Louis Smith does not seem to fit this mitigating category.

Instead, Smith seems to suffer from a violent temper. There is no evidence of a new, foreign value structure in him. It seems more fitting to describe him as a violent person than as a docile person who is mysteriously displaced occasionally. Violent persons aren't always violent; they don't roam about smashing people and objects willy-nilly. They are called violent in light of their disposition to translate their aggressive feelings into destructive acts. Although the acts of violence are intermittent, they are no more foreign to the personality than are the intermittent risky acts of the courageous man. The category "uncontrollable aggression" holds the danger of treating our ruling passions as foreign to us, when it is the very order of those passions which defines us. Louis Smith is a passionately violent man, not a victim of violent passion.

You can easily imagine the grotesque consequences of classifying persons by their ruling passions: "uncontrollable piety," "uncontrollable loyalty," "uncontrollable humor," "uncontrollable charity," "uncontrollable industry," "uncontrollable gluttony," "uncontrollable wanderlust." You can picture the long lines outside a clinic, each uncontrollable person waiting for his medication under the directions of the state. Even the poor doctors at the Lafayette Clinic might face treatment of "uncontrollable inquiry."

Of course, there is a sense in which all of us are afflicted by uncontrollable passions. If there is a hierarchy of values within us, those on top will not be checked by other values. While your love of money may be tempered by your concern for your reputation so that you do not steal, what tempers your concern for reputation? If nothing does, then you are "suffering" from "uncontrollable concern for reputation." This sort of suffering is quite different from that caused by viral infection. Viral infection invades the body and is not integral to it. Uncontrollable passions are not invaders, but components of personality.

In sum, there are people who are not the victims of "uncontrollable aggression." They are neither confused nor displaced. They are, instead, violent, dangerous persons. Hatred and contempt occupy an unusually high position in their personality; when hatred and contempt "speak up," they are honored rather than suppressed. This is not sickness, but evil.

The state errs in sending people like this to hospitals. They should be tried for their actions. Persons of this type might show that they reject their own violence by seeking radical treatment during the periods of calm. If, for example, they request incarceration or risky surgery so that they might not be a danger to others, they would show their will to control their worst side. These kinds of efforts could be clear indicators of the value these persons place upon the well-being of others. If, however, such persons take no strong measures to neutralize the danger that they present, they are responsible for their behavior.

Finally, in the case of Louis Smith, his release on grounds of cure as well as the court's ruling on "voluntary" assent to treatment depend upon a mistaken view of punishment. The biblical notion is retributive, not rehabilitative. Since it is doubtful that Smith was ill to begin with, the declaration of cure is in error. And since he murdered a nurse, the declaration of cure is irrelevant. If, happily, he were to rearrange his priorities, becoming nonviolent, there would still be no grounds for release from prison. He is not there in quarantine but in guilt. The offense has its due, and it must not be thought that this is a hard and inhuman approach. On the contrary, it is the most charitable approach; the alternatives are more dangerous and irresponsible.

Similarly, the practice of tying parole to reform by surgery is unfortunate. No doubt, the attractive prospect of release could be coercive. But the issue of voluntary and involuntary treatment should not even arise. At most, under a retributive view, psychosurgery would make the prisoner a more placid prisoner, not a free man. If he chooses to reform himself in prison, this is marvelous. What better place for ministry?

Conclusion

When introduced to the metric system, I had very little sympathy for it. Internally, the system was a beautiful combination of multiples of ten, but the fit with our ordinary weights and measures was uncomfortable. The meter came to 39.37 inches, the liter to 1.0567 quarts, and the kilogram to 2.2046 pounds. If only the liter had been a quart and the meter a yard, then the metric system would have been reasonable rather than perverse.

It did not take much reflection to see that the problem lay with me and not with meters. It was not that metric measurement ill-suited human purposes or that the system was unwieldy. Its only offense was its indifference to the old categorial system. I expected meters to be "answerable" to yards. But, with a shift in perspective I was struck by the strangeness of yards. They are, after all, .9144 of a meter. What a curious measurement, the yard.

I recall these thoughts for the sake of analogy. This book's proposals are also indifferent to some commonly accepted concepts and so may seem perverse. Is it a conservative or liberal theory? It's hard to say. It takes a fairly hard line on punishment and repudiates reverse discrimination. In these respects, the theory can be more easily identified with the interests of conservatives. But then it urges substantial welfare and health-care programs, rejects strategic nuclear warfare, and allows for a good deal of state control over the use of expendable resources. These positions smack of liberalism.

As for civil liberties, it's not clear into which category the theory falls. There are radical libertarians among both conservatives and liberals. The position on pornography seems more liberal while the one on suicide seems more conservative. Conservatives oppose big, paternalistic government, but some of the most stalwart civil libertarians have been liberals. So the liberal-conservative distinction is not clean-cut in ordinary use. Still, there is enough of a distinction to make the concepts workable. They provide, if you will, one system of weights and measures.

The matrix theory doesn't honor this popular distinction. It clashes with the ordinary system of measurement. It finds both truth and error in each camp, and suggests a different grouping. And so it may appear perverse. But just as with the metric system, there can be a shift in perspective which alters the standard of perversity. Both conservativism and liberalism can come to seem strange, forced, and unfortunate in some respects. It is no failing to depart here and there from the conservative or the liberal line. For here and there, those lines are ill-conceived.

Finally, this work has been both a guess and a prospectus. The Bible resists cocksure interpretation on these matters. Yet, we must choose among political candidates, accept or resist the draft, and decide whether to sign a petition that a pornographic book store be closed. The issues are impossible to avoid. So we guess. We make the best one we can and continually check it against both Scripture and life. I hope that the "matrix guess" will strike the reader as a reasonable one.

No doubt, a good deal of work remains. A host of concepts and principles invite development, clarification, and adjustment. We have only a sketch here. Because it is a sketch or prospectus, we can grasp the image in short order. If it is a bad one, it can be quickly discarded or demolished. If it is a good one, then we can make time for the necessary refinements.